INTRODUCTION TO FACTOR ANALYSIS

What It Is and How To Do It

Jae-On Kim

Charles W. Mueller

Series: Quantitative Applications
in the Social Sciences

SAGE UNIVERSITY PAPER

13

SAGE UNIVERSITY PAPERS

Series: Quantitative Applications in the Social Sciences

Series Editor: **John L. Sullivan**, University of Minnesota

Editorial Advisory Board

James Fennessey, Johns Hopkins University
Lawrence S. Mayer, University of Pennsylvania
Richard G. Niemi, University of Rochester
Ronald E. Weber, Louisiana State University

Publisher
Sara Miller McCune, Sage Publications, Inc.

Series / Number 07-013

INTRODUCTION TO FACTOR ANALYSIS

What it is and How To Do It

JAE-ON KIM
CHARLES W. MUELLER

University of Iowa

S SAGE PUBLICATIONS / Beverly Hills / London

For information address:

SAGE Publications, Inc.
275 South Beverly Drive
Beverly Hills, California 90212

SAGE Publications Ltd
28 Banner Street
London EC1Y 8QE

International Standard Book Number 0-8039-1165-3

Library of Congress Catalog Card No. L.C. 78-64331

NINTH PRINTING, 1982

When citing a professional paper, please use the proper form. Remember to cite the correct Sage University Paper series title and include the paper number. One of the two following formats can be adapted (depending on the style manual used):

(1) IVERSEN, GUDMUND R. and NORPOTH, HELMUT (1976) "Analysis of Variance." Sage University Paper series on Quantitative Applications in the Social Sciences, 07-001. Beverly Hills and London: Sage Pubns.

OR

(2) Iversen, Gudmund R. and Norpoth, Helmut. 1976. *Analysis of Variance.* Sage University Paper series on Quantitative Applications in the Social Sciences, series no. 07-001. Beverly Hills and London: Sage Publications.

CONTENTS

Editor's Introduction

This volume, along with its companion, *FACTOR ANALYSIS: STATISTICAL METHODS AND PRACTICAL ISSUES,* deals with one of the more widely used methods of data reduction in social science research.* In *AN INTRODUCTION TO FACTOR ANALYSIS: WHAT IT IS AND HOW TO DO IT,* Jae-On Kim and Charles W. Mueller provide a guide to the perplexed. One of the most widely used techniques in quantitative social science, factor analysis is also one of the least understood. Textbooks abound on the topic, most requiring a great deal of mathematical sophistication. Yet, social scientists who employ the technique differ widely in their own preferences among such volumes; some books are too technical, others concentrate on too esoteric variants on factor analysis, some fail to make critical distinctions among types of factor analysis, while others simply contain mathematical errors. The specialist is too often frustrated in selecting from among these volumes; the nonspecialist may throw up his (her) arms in frustration and let the prewritten computer programs make the critical decisions.

In this first volume, the authors discuss the rationale for doing factor analytic studies. They discuss situations in which a set of variables is marked by virtually zero correlations, and those in which there are strong intercorrelations among the variables. Exploratory factor analysis attempts to reduce a set of, say ten variables, into two or three underlying "factors." Confirmatory factor analysis, on the other hand, posits that there are, say, two underlying factors for a set of ten variables and then seeks to determine whether this hypothesis does hold. The authors relate these types of factor analysis to causal inferences (path analysis) and discuss the theoretical assumptions one at least implicitly makes when using the technique.** In their exposition, the authors discuss some of the underlying mathematics behind the technique (including the relationship of correlation, variance, and covariance to the factor model). The mathematics is generally kept at an introductory level; whenever a more advanced concept is introduced, it is related to simple algebra.

---

*For another method of data reduction, see Joseph B. Kruskal and Myron Wish, *Multidimensional Scaling* (1977). Another paper, also in this series, which builds upon the factor analysis model is Mark Levine (1977), *Canonical Analysis and Factor Comparison.*
**See Herbert B. Asher (1976), *Causal Modeling,* in this series.

The authors assume in this first monograph that the data are measured without error; this assumption is dropped in the second volume. They also analyze problems of data collection and preparation for input to the most commonly used computer programs to perform factor analysis. (An extended analysis of how to use the SPSS package and more limited examples from other programs are also presented.) Kim and Mueller also discuss the problem of factor rotation, i.e., the "adjusting" of a particular configuration of data in the hope that it will be more meaningful in empirical applications. A brief discussion of sampling variability, selection bias, measurement errors, and minor factors is presented. Most useful is a set of questions and answers to some of the most puzzling problems associated with factor analysis; a glossary is also a unique contribution to this volume. Kim and Mueller have provided a readable, technically sound, and practical guide to learning the elements of factor analysis. The interested reader is referred to their companion volume, *FACTOR ANALYSIS: STATISTICAL METHODS AND PRACTICAL ISSUES*, for a more detailed explication of these techniques and to a forthcoming volume on *MULTIPLE INDICATORS* for an examination of maximum likelihood factor analysis.***

Factor analysis has been used in economics to derive a set of uncorrelated variables for further analysis when the use of highly intercorrelated variables may yield misleading results in regression analysis. Political scientists have compared the attributes of nations on a variety of political and socioeconomic variables in an attempt to determine what characteristics are most important in classifying nations (e.g., wealth and size);**** sociologists have determined "friendship groups" by examining which people associate most frequently with each other (and not with other individuals). Psychologists and educators have used the technique to determine how people perceive different "stimuli" and categorize them into different reponse sets, e.g., how different elements of language are interrelated.

As the authors indicate, these papers cannot possibly cover all of the aspects of factor analysis, since there are new developments constantly emerging in this area. However, if the reader can develop a more systematic knowledge of how the technique is to be used and what assumptions one is at least implicitly making, then these papers will have served their purpose well.

—E. M. Uslaner, Series Editor

***John L. Sullivan and Stanley Feldman (forthcoming), *Multiple Indicators*, in this series.
****See Rudolph J. Rummel, *The Dimensions of Nations* (Beverly Hills, CA: Sage Publications, 1972).

I. INTRODUCTION

Basic Orientation

In recent years, factor analysis has become accessible to a wider circle of researchers and students, primarily due to the development of high speed computers and the packaged computer programs (e.g., BMD, DATATEXT, OSIRIS, SAS AND SPSS). This has resulted in a large group of users who do not have enough mathematical training to follow standard texts on the subject (e.g., Harman, 1976; Horst, 1965; Lawley and Maxwell, 1971; Mulaik, 1972) but are nevertheless eager to explore and exploit the potentials of the method for their own research.

The audience we have in mind is this growing population of consumers of factor analysis who are willing to let the computers do the work and let the specialists worry about the statistical and computational problems, but who are willing to invest some effort to gain a firmer grasp of its conceptual foundations in order to apply the method correctly and creatively. In addition, because we anticipate our typical reader to be a nonspecialist, but a potentially active user of the method, we believe the numerous practical problems often encountered should be addressed.

Although this is an elementary introduction to factor analysis, it is not an ordinary introductory text. The assumption which guided our writing is that what is most obvious to an expert is often most obscure to a novice. Therefore, we have discussed in greater detail than usual the fundamental assumptions and logical foundations of factor analysis. It has been a challenge for us to attempt to cover the fundamentals in greater detail than usual and at the same time discuss the practical issues which users continually confront. It is possible in principle to propose such a book because the logical (mathematical) foundation of factor analysis can be separated from the statistical solutions, because the method's logical foundation is straightforward and easy to understand, *and* because an understanding of this foundation will be the basis for the intelligent use of the method. In short, we believe many of the statistical issues in factor analysis are truly subsidiary, and placing emphasis on them diverts attention away from the logical foundation and results in a confused and tentative potential user.

The difference between what we call logical and statistical may not be clear at this early stage; therefore, some comments are in order. Factor

AUTHORS' NOTE: *We wish to express our appreciation and thanks to the numerous people who helped make the completion of this manuscript possible. In particular, computer assistance was provided by James Meeks-Johnson, Chia Hsing Lu, and Gayle Scriven. David Kenney, James Rabjohn, Elaine Black, and James Duane offered advice and suggestions on an earlier draft of the manuscript. A special thanks should go to Eric Uslaner, Lawrence Mayer, and an anonymous reviewer for their useful comments and advice.*

analysis assumes that the observed (measured) variables are linear combinations of some underlying source variables (or factors). That is, it assumes the existence of a system of underlying factors and a system of observed variables. There is a certain correspondence between these two systems and factor analysis "exploits" this correspondence to arrive at conclusions about the factors. For instance, the mathematical (logical) properties of the correspondence are such that one causal system of factors always leads to a unique correlation system of observed variables, but not vice versa. Therefore, only under very limited conditions can one unequivocally determine the underlying causal structure among the factors from the correlations among the observed variables. This fundamental indeterminancy in factor analysis is due to the indeterminancy inherent in making *inferences* about the causal structure from the correlational structure; it is a logical or mathematical indeterminancy. However, there also are problems of a different nature. As an example, in practice one has to contend with uncertainties introduced by sampling and measurement errors. How to estimate the underlying population parameters from the examination of samples under these uncertainties is a *statistical* problem. Our position is to let statisticians worry about providing us the most efficient ways of estimating population parameters as well as answers to other statistical problems. The logical issues we will address.

We do not and cannot promise not to rely on mathematics, but our use of mathematics will be limited primarily (but not entirely) to simple algebra, and we strongly recommend to the readers that they make an honest attempt to follow the algebra presented. In anticipation that some readers might be discouraged by the mere appearance of the word mathematical, we emphasize once again that our approach is not mathematically rigorous. We will try to explain such terms as "factors," and "variable," "linear combination of variables," and "linear causal systems" by way of illustration. With regard to the statistical background expected of the reader, we will assume some familiarity with correlation and regression analysis. We will rely on path analysis to aid in illustrating the factor models we refer to. Path diagrams readily allow for the visual portrayal of the underlying causal relationships among factors and observed variables. We will explain the essentials of path diagrams as we go along. The use of path diagrams as a means of expressing linear relationships and the requisite assumptions about them should not prove difficult to those who have had no previous exposure to path analysis. (For those wishing a more complete introduction we recommend the Asher [1976] volume in this series or one of the standard references; see Duncan, 1966; Land, 1969; Li, 1975).

What is Factor Analysis?

Factor analysis refers to a variety of statistical techniques whose common objective is to represent a set of variables in terms of a smaller number of hypothetical variables. To make our introductory discussion of factor analysis more concrete, suppose we have interviewed one thousand individuals who are randomly selected from the population, and have asked them many questions about their political opinions on taxation, labor laws, civil rights issues, and so on. The responses to these questions then constitute observed variables.

In general, the first step of the analysis involves an examination of the interrelationships among these variables. Suppose that we use the correlation coefficient as a measure of association and have prepared a table of correlations. Inspection of the correlation matrix may show that there are positive relationships among these variables, and that the relationships within some subsets of variables are higher than those between the subsets. A factor analytic approach may then be used to address whether these observed correlations can be explained by the existence of a small number of hypothetical variables. For instance, we might ask whether there is a liberal-conservative continuum which characterizes the general political outlook of the people. Or we might conjecture that there may be some subdivisions of liberalism-conservatism. For example, it is quite possible that economic issues may tap a somewhat different dimension than civil rights issues. We might then consider whether these potential subdivisions really do emerge from the data. These kinds of questions are best handled by factor analytic techniques.

At one extreme, the researcher may not have any idea as to how many underlying dimensions there are for the given data. Therefore, factor analysis may be used as an expedient way of ascertaining the minimum number of hypothetical factors that can account for the observed covariation, and as a means of exploring the data for possible data reduction. This form of use is *exploratory*, with probably the majority of the applications in the social sciences belonging to this category.

But the use of factor analysis need not be confined to exploring the underlying dimensions of the data. Depending upon the knowledge of the researcher, the method can be used as a means of testing specific hypotheses. For instance, the researcher may anticipate or hypothesize that there are two different underlying dimensions *and* that certain variables belong to one dimension while others belong to the second. If factor analysis is used to test this expectation, then it is used as a means of confirming a certain hypothesis, not as a means of exploring underlying dimensions. Thus, it is referred to as *confirmatory* factor analysis.

The division between the two uses is not always clearcut. For instance, it is possible that the researcher may specify that there will be, say, two factors but may not anticipate exactly what variables will represent each. Or to illustrate one of the numerous strategies that can be employed, the researcher may use one-half of the sample to explore the possible factor structure, and then use the other half of the sample to test the factorial hypothesis that was developed from the examination of the first half.

Factor analysis is used not only as a formal method of ascertaining underlying factor structure, but is also often used as a heuristic device. For example, assume the researcher is certain that on the basis of previous research or strong theory there are two separate dimensions of liberalism— one mainly concerned with the economic issues and the other with civil rights issues. This researcher is interested primarily in constructing a scale of economic liberalism (to be used as a variable in further analysis), but is uncertain whether the opinions about providing financial aid to unwed mothers reflect the dimension of economic liberalism, or is better subsumed under the civil rights dimension. Here factor analysis may be used as a means of checking out the meaning of a particular variable or variables. The researcher might find out through factor analysis that variables X_1, X_2, X_3, clearly reflect economic liberalism, and variables X_5 and X_6 reflect social liberalism, but that variable X_4 is related to both dimensions, and its meaning, given the immediate research objective of constructing the scale of economic liberalism, is ambiguous. Therefore, X_4 could be dropped from the index of economic liberalism.

Without going into the details of the method, it would not make much sense to elaborate further about its potential uses for research. We merely state for now that it can be used in a variety of research situations, and that proper use of factor analysis does not require mastering complex statistical techniques but rests primarily on an understanding of its conceptual and logical foundation.

Doing Factor Analysis

It is one thing to study and grasp the principles of factor analysis and it is another to apply it to actual data. Except for very unrealistic hypothetical data, it is impractical to do factor analysis without the help of modern computers. Because only a very small minority would have the expertise to write the appropriate program, it is almost imperative that one rely on some existing computer program. Fortunately, there are some well-known and widely used general purpose computer packages that contain factor analysis programs. Unfortunately, however, there are so many methods and variants of factor analysis that we cannot cover them here, nor will any single computer package include them all. Furthermore, there appears to be no end in sight regarding new modifications and improvements. Hence, the program available to the user may not be up-to-date or, if up-to-date, may seem too complicated to use. For most factor analysis problems, one does not have to use the most up-to-date version nor does one need to know all of the complexities in order to use the newest versions. We will show that it is possible to ignore most of these complications, especially at the early stages of learning, and obtain the desired results by preparing a minimum number of computer control statements.

It is our belief that being able to apply factor analysis to fairly complex and real problems right from the beginning not only helps the user to become acquainted with the technique quickly, but also diminishes the need for learning the actual algorithms that are involved. We do recommend and, therefore, will illustrate, the use of existing packaged computer programs. It is expected that the reader will attempt to use one of these programs as early as is possible. However, as much as we emphasize the fact that reliance on an existing computer program is a fact of life, we also expect that the user will consult this volume and the companion volume, *Factor Analysis: Statistical Methods and Practical Issues,* University Paper, 07-014, in order to develop a deeper understanding of factor analysis.

The general purpose programs to be illustrated are BMD, OSIRIS, SAS, and SPSS. It should be noted, however, that we have used these packages for illustrative purposes and it is not necessary that one has access to these particular ones. Any program can serve the purpose, but to be successful in learning factor analysis, one must be prepared to spend some time learning how to use at least one factor analysis computer program.

General Outline of Presentation

The discussion of factor analysis is presented in two volumes. In the first volume, coverage is confined to a description of the conceptual foundations of factor analysis, and the use of computer programs as a means of obtaining basic solutions. Discussion of various methods of extraction and rotation, as well as more advanced topics, is included in the companion volume.

More specifically, the first volume is organized into three main sections. The section following this introduction, Section II: Mathematical Foundations of Factor Analysis, deals with the logical foundations of the technique. In order to present this material in the simplest manner possible, we will assume that we are creating the world according to the factor analytic scheme. In this hypothetical world there will be no errors of sampling or measurement. Here we will introduce the basic concepts of variable and factor, variance and covariance, and linear causal system.

The properties of the linear system will be examined rather thoroughly by way of illustrations and mathematical derivations pertaining to the simplest possible situations. We will also examine the sources of logical uncertainties and ways of handling these uncertainties by adopting some fundamental postulates of factor analysis.

In Section III we provide a discussion of how factor analysis is actually conducted. We begin by describing the major steps involved in using the technique, and then illustrate these steps by analyzing error-free data. Descriptions of how to use four of the readily available packaged computer programs are presented. Finally, we describe briefly the complications introduced when real data are analyzed, leaving the treatment of specific and technical issues to the companion volume. Also included in this volume are (1) a brief introduction to the books, articles, and computer programs on factor analysis, (2) a glossary of difficult terms used in this volume, and (3) references to the basic literature.

In the second volume, *Factor Analysis: Statistical Methods and Practical Issues,* we shift our focus to the statistical issues. Building on the conceptual foundations presented in the first volume, we present in order, (1) several standard methods of extracting initial factors, (2) numerous methods of orthogonal and oblique rotations, (3) the rules for determining the number of common factors to retain and interpret, (4) introduction to confirmatory factor analysis, and (5) methods of constructing factor scales. In addition, several practical problems that most social scientists are likely to encounter are discussed in a question and answer format. A glossary and references appear at the end, as in the first volume.

II. LOGICAL FOUNDATIONS OF FACTOR ANALYSIS

Fundamental Concepts of Factor Analysis

FACTORS AND VARIABLES

Factor Analysis is based on the fundamental assumption that some underlying factors, which are smaller in number than the number of observed variables, are responsible for the covariation among the observed variables. To illustrate the model, let us examine the simplest case where one underlying common factor is responsible for the covariation between two observed variables. Such an assumption may be expressed in a path analytic causal diagram as follows:

This diagram implies that X_1 is a weighted sum of F and U_1, and X_2 is a weighted sum of F and U_2. Because F is common to both X_1 and X_2, it may be called a common factor; likewise, because U_1 and U_2 are unique

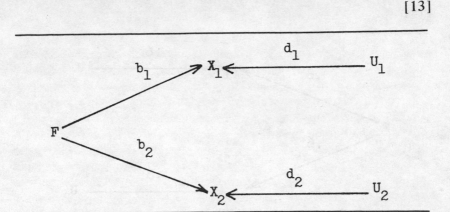

Figure 1: Path Model for a Two-Variable, One-Common Factor Model

to each observed variable, they may be referred to as unique factors. In algebraic form, the diagram implies the following two equations:

$$X_1 = b_1 F + d_1 U_1$$

$$X_2 = b_2 F + d_2 U_2$$

[1]

Furthermore, the diagram also indicates that there is no covariation between F and U_1, between F and U_2, or between U_1 and U_2. That is,

$$\text{cov}(F, U_1) = \text{cov}(F, U_2) = \text{cov}(U_1, U_2) = 0.$$ [2]

The preceding three equations, then, together describe a factor analytic linear system shown in Figure 1.

For those who might have trouble following the path diagram or imagining such an abstract system, we will present a concrete example. Assume that there are three source variables, F, U_1 and U_2, and eight cases (or entities) as in Table 1. Each source variable has two possible values, either 1 or −1, and they are uncorrelated with each other. Suppose now that you are asked to create variables from these source materials according to a set of rules. These specific rules are indicated by the causal diagram in Figure 2: these rules are to create X_1 by combining F and U_1 with weights of .8 and .6 respectively, and to create X_2 by combining F and U_2 with weights .6 and .8.

Such a set of operations can be summed up either by the following two equations:

$$X_1 = .8F + .6U_1$$

$$X_2 = .6F + .8U_2$$

or by the path diagram in Figure 2.

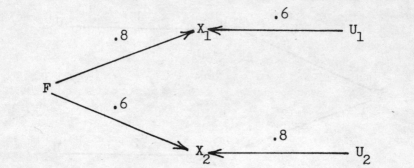

Figure 2: Path Model for a Two-Variable, One-Common Factor Model (consistent with Table 1 Data)

The path diagram actually contains more information than the two equations; in the diagram, the absence of direct or indirect connections between the source variables indicates no correlations among them, whereas the relationships among the source variables are left unspecified in the two equations. In order to indicate that variables X_1 and X_2 are created by the use of uncorrelated source variables, one must add the following conditions to the equations:

$$\text{cov}(F, U_i) = \text{cov}(U_i, U_j) = 0.$$

TABLE 1
Illustration of Factors and Variables:
Two-Variables, One-Common Factor

| Cases | Source Variables[a] | | | Observed Variables | |
	F	U_1	U_2	$X_1 = .8F + .6U_1$	$X_2 = .6F + .8U_2$
1	1	1	1	1.4	1.4
2	1	1	-1	1.4	-0.2
3	1	-1	1	0.2	1.4
4	1	-1	-1	0.2	-0.2
5	-1	1	1	-0.2	0.2
6	-1	1	-1	-0.2	-1.4
7	-1	-1	1	-1.4	0.2
8	-1	-1	-1	-1.4	1.4

a. We use this unrealistic scoring of the source variables to simplify our computations on this basic factor model.

The variables created by applying these rules are presented in the fourth and fifth columns of Table 1.

If we treat X_1 and X_2 as observed variables, and F, U_1 and U_2 as unobserved variables, we have the simplest one common factor model.

Note that there are more factors (Fs and Us) than observed variables (Xs), but only the factor F is common to both X_1 and X_2 and, therefore, the number of common factors is smaller than the number of observed variables. Note also that in creating Xs we have used only certain types of mathematical operations: (1) multiplying the source variables by constants, and (2) adding these products. We did not multiply or divide one factor by the other. In technical language, we are using only linear operations and, hence are creating a linear system.

We will conclude this section by describing how the terms, variables and factors, are used and how they are related. A variable is a concept which has two or more values. In the example, F, U_1, and U_2 all have two values. We assume that these variables are given to us and we are not concerned with their sources. X_1 and X_2, created from the source variables through the linear operations, are also variables—each having four possible values. In order to indicate that the source variables are usually unobserved by the researcher and that the observed variables are created out of them, we call such source variables underlying *factors*. Since none of us really participates in the creation of real world variables by applying the kind of operations described above, we often call these source variables hypothetical constructs, hypothetical variables, or hypothetical factors. Of these factors, those that are involved in the creation of more than one observed variable are called common factors; those that are used in creating only one observed variable are called unique factors.

VARIANCE, COVARIANCE AND CORRELATION

There are two properties of a variable that play important roles in statistics: mean and variance. The mean (or expectation of a variable) indicates the central tendency of a variable, and the variance indicates the degree of dispersion (or variability). They are defined as:

$$\text{Mean} = \Sigma(X_i)/N \qquad (i = 1, 2, \ldots, N)$$

$$= E(X) = \bar{X} \qquad\qquad [3]$$

$$\text{Variance} = \Sigma[X_i - E(X)]^2/N \qquad (i = 1, 2, \ldots, N)$$

$$= E[X - E(X)]^2 = V_x. \qquad\qquad [4]$$

We will use the expectation notation E as an abbreviation for adding all the values and dividing that sum by the total number of cases.[1] If the variable is normally distributed, then these two statistics are sufficient to characterize the whole probability distribution of the variable.

The five variables in our example (F, U_1, U_2, X_1, and X_2) all have means of zero and variances of 1. Such variables are called *normed* variables or *standardized* variables. Any variable can be transformed into such a standardized variable by simply subtracting the mean from the observed values and dividing the resulting values by the square root of the variance. Therefore, we do not lose any generality by dealing with only standardized variables.

In characterizing linear relationships between variables, the concept of covariance plays a crucial role. Its definition is:

$$\text{cov}\,(X, Y) = \Sigma\,[(X_i - \bar{X})\,(Y_i - \bar{Y})]/N \qquad (i = 1, 2, \ldots, N)$$

$$= E\,[(X - \bar{X})\,(Y - \bar{Y})] \qquad [5]$$

Note that cases falling at the mean of each variable will not contribute to the magnitude of covariance; if a case has a higher value than the mean on one variable but a lower value on another, it will contribute a negative value to the covariance; if a case has either higher values or lower values on both variables, it will increase the covariance. Thus, covariance measures the extent to which values of one variable tend to covary with values of another variable. The *covariance* between standardized variables (with a mean of 0 and a variance of 1) has a special name: *correlation coefficient* or *product-moment* (*Pearson's*) *correlation coefficient:*

$$\text{cov}\,(X, Y) = E(XY) \qquad [6]$$

if $\bar{X} = \bar{Y} = 0$;

$$= r_{xy}, \qquad [7]$$

if $V_x = V_y = 1$.

If one variable can be expressed as a linear function of the other, as in $Y = a + bx$ (or as a linear combination of the other), the correlation coefficient will be either 1 or -1, and the coefficient of determination (R^2) will be 1. If the two variables are statistically independent, the magnitude of correlation will be zero. Otherwise, the magnitude of r will vary between $+1$ and -1. (If the distribution is bivariate normal, the means, the variances, and the correlation between the two completely specify the bivariate distribution.)

It is important to note that the notion of covariation is independent of the underlying causal structure; two variables can covary either because one variable is a cause of the other or both variables share at least one common cause, or both. In the linear system shown in Figure 1, there is covariation between X_1 and F because F is one of the source variables. However, there is covariation between X_1 and X_2 because both share a common source variable (F).

LINEAR COMBINATIONS AND DERIVATIONS
OF VARIANCE AND COVARIANCE

It is our belief that one of the main reasons why many people fail to grasp the mathematical foundation of factor analysis is lack of understanding of several basic characteristics of linear combinations of variables. Our task in this section is to aid in increasing that understanding. We will examine the mathematical basis of the covariance structure (or correlation structure) or linear systems (such as the one common factor model shown in Figures 1 and 2). We alert the reader in advance that this section will probably be one of the most difficult mathematically, but it is one that is crucial to understanding the mathematical basis for factor analysis. Do not despair prematurely; the algebra involved is actually not that difficult and, once mastered, the remainder of this paper will be much easier.

The derivation of the amount of variance in X_1 and the covariance between X_1 and F is possible due to the fact that X_1 is a linear combination of F and U_1 (i.e., $X_1 = b_1 F + d_1 U_1$). Since we assumed that F and the Us all have means of zero and variances of 1, these derivations can be simplified, without loss of generality. (In fact, the derivations would remain the same even if there is an additional constant as in $X_1 = a + b_1 F + d_1 U_1$.) The variance of X_1, Var (X_1), may be expressed as

$$\text{Var } (X_1) = E(X_1 - \overline{X}_1)^2$$

(which is given by the definition of variance, as in equation 4)

$$= E(X_1)^2$$

(which is obtained by assuming that the mean of X_1 is zero)

$$= E[b_1 F + d_1 U_1]^2.$$

(which is obtained by expressing X_1 in terms of the source variables) Through simple expansion this may be rewritten as

$$= E[b_1^2 F^2 + d_1^2 U_1^2 + 2b_1 d_1 F U_1],$$

and by knowing that the expectation of a constant is the constant, the constants may be factored out as follows,

$$= b_1^2 E[F^2] + d_1^2 E[U_1^2] + 2b_1 d_1 E[F U_1],$$

which allows us to recognize that the terms associated with the expectation notation have previously been defined as either variances or covariances. Hence, the variance of X_1 has been decomposed as follows

$$= b_1^2 \text{Var}(F) + d_1^2 \text{Var}(U_1) + 2b_1 d_1 \text{Cov}(F, U_1). \qquad [8]$$

Equation 8 is a general formula dealing with a case in which one variable is a linear combination of two source variables. In words, the resulting variance in X_1 is given by the sum of (1) the variance of F times the square of the weight associated with F, (2) the variance of U_1 times the square of the weight for U_1, and (3) two times the covariance between the source variables multiplied by the two respective weights. (If the preceding definitions and derivations are new to you, we recommend that you go over this material again. You must understand these basics if the following material is to be meaningful.)

Fortunately, equation 8 simplifies if the source variables are standardized and the covariance ~~between~~ the source variables is zero (as in our example above): ^among^

$$\text{Variance } (X_1) = b_1^2 \text{var}(F) + d_1^2 \text{var}(U_1), \qquad [9]$$

if cov $(F, U_1) = 0$.

Here the variance in X_1 is decomposed into only two parts: a component determined by the common factor F and a component determined by the unique factor U_1. The decomposition becomes even simpler if variables are all in standardized form:

$$\text{var } (X_1) = b_1^2 + d_1^2 = 1 \qquad [10]$$

if var $(F) = \text{var } (U_1) = \text{var } (X_1) = 1$ and cov $(F, U_1) = 0$.

Likewise, Var (X_2) can be decomposed as

$$\text{var } (X_2) = b_2^2 + d_2^2.$$

In our example, we have contrived data and coefficients (weights) in such a way that var $(F) = \text{var } (U_i) = \text{var } (X_i) = 1$ (that is, all the variables are in standardized form) and cov $(F, U_j) = 0$. Consequently,

$$\text{var } (X_1) = 1 = b_1^2 + d_1^2 = (.8)^2 + (.6)^2 = .64 + .36$$

$$\text{var } (X_2) = 1 = b_2^2 + d_2^2 = (.6)^2 + (.8)^2 = .36 + .64$$

Therefore, in our example, the proportion of variance in X_1 determined by the common factor is .64 while the proportion determined by the unique factor is .36.

In similar fashion the covariance between a factor and an observed variable may be derived:

$$\text{Cov}(F, X_1) = E[(F - \overline{F})(X_1 - \overline{X}_1)]$$

(from the basic definition of covariance, as given in equation 5)

$$= E[FX_1]$$

(which is possible because we have assumed $\overline{F} = \overline{X}_1 = 0$)

$$= E[(F)(b_1 F + d_1 U_1)]$$

(which is obtained by expressing X_1 in terms of its source variables)

$$= b_1 E[F^2] + d_1 E[FU_1]$$

(by recognizing that the constants may be factored out)

$$= b_1 \text{Var}(F) + d_1 \text{Cov}(FU_1) \tag{11}$$

(which follows from the basic definitions of variance and covariance). Equation 11 is a general formula dealing with any situation in which a variable is a linear combination of two source variables. In words, the covariance between a source variable and the resulting variable is given by the sum of (1) the linear weight times the variance of the source variable, and (2) the linear weight of the other source variable times the covariance between the two source variables.

When the source variables are independent of each other, equation 11 simplifies to

$$\text{Cov}(F, X_1) = b_1 \text{Var}(F) \tag{12}$$

and when the source variables have unit variances, it further simplifies to

$$\text{Cov}(F, X_1) = b_1. \tag{13}$$

Furthermore, if the observed variable X_1 is also in standardized form, then

$$\text{Cov}(F, X_1) = r_{Fx_1} = b_1 = \beta_1. \tag{14}$$

That is, the covariance is equivalent to the correlation and the linear weight b_1, which is equivalent to a standardized regression coefficient β_1. (Here the independent variable is the factor, and the dependent variable is the observed variable.) Likewise cov $(F, X_2) = r_{Fx_2} = b_2 = \beta_2$. Furthermore, the correlation between X_1 and the unique factor U_1, can be derived in exactly the same way: cov $(X_1, U_1) = r_{x_1 u} = d_1$ = standardized regression coefficient.

We may now consider the relationships we have examined thus far in order to interpret the correlation coefficient in the context of factor analysis. In Figure 2 we may now identify the weights .8 and .6 as standardized regression coefficients. At the same time, we know that given the particular linear system in the example, they are also equivalent to correlations between the created variable and the source variables. The squares of these correlations (.64 and .36) correctly describe the proportion of the variance in X_1 and X_2, which is *determined* by the common factor. The square of the correlation coefficient is traditionally known as the *coefficient of determination*, a term which is apt if we have a causal system as shown in Figure 1. But it is used, in general, simply as a means of stating the degree of linear relationship without any reference to the underlying causal relationship. (At this point, we encourage the reader to calculate these coefficients using the data shown in Table 1. Such an exercise will provide an immediate check on whether the reader really understands how the concepts and definitions presented thus far are applied. As we said earlier these elementary concepts are essential to understanding the mathematical model underlying factor analysis. Some results of calculations are shown in Table 2 for those who wish to check their own computations.)

Finally, we derive the covariance between X_1 and X_2:

$$\text{Cov } (X_1, X_2) = E[X_1 - \bar{X}_1)(X_2 - \bar{X}_2)]$$

(from the definition of covariance as given in equation 5)

$$= E[b_1 F + d_1 U_1)(b_2 F + d_2 U_2)]$$

(because we have assumed the variables are standardized with means equal to zero, and by expressing the Xs in terms of source variables)

$$= E[b_1 b_2 F^2 + b_1 d_2 FU_2 + b_2 d_1 FU_1 + d_1 d_2 U_1 U_2]$$

(by simple algebraic expansion)

$$= b_1 b_2 \text{var}(F) + b_1 d_2 \text{cov}(F_1 U_2) + b_2 d_1 \text{cov}(F,U_1) \qquad [15]$$
$$+ d_1 d_2 \text{cov}(U_1,U_2)$$

(by separating out the constants and recognizing that the remaining expected values are either variances or covariances).

Equation 15 is appropriate for the general case. However, it simplifies to the following if all the covariance terms vanish (as is the case for our hypothetical data):

$$\text{cov}(X_1, X_2) = b_1 b_2 \text{var}(F). \qquad [16]$$

And this simplifies further,

$$\text{cov}(X_1, X_2) = r_{X_1 X_2} = b_1 b_2 = \beta_1 \beta_2 \qquad [17]$$

if all the variables are standardized. In words, the covariance between two observed variables sharing one common factor is equivalent to the variance of the factor times the two respective linear weights involved. When all the variables are in standardized form, the correlation between two observed variables sharing one common factor is given by the multiplication of two standardized regression coefficients or two correlations between the observed variables and the common factor.

RECAPITULATION:
Factor Loadings, Correlations, and Causal Diagrams

Referring back to Figures 1 and 2, we will review the concepts and definitions examined thus far. If all the variables (both hypothetical and observed) are standardized to have unit variance, the linear weights, b_1 and b_2 in Figure 1, are known as *standardized regression coefficients* (in regression analysis), path coefficients (in causal analysis), or factor loadings (in factor analysis). Factor loadings are equivalent to correlations between factors and variables where only a single common factor is involved, or in the case where multiple common factors are orthogonal to each other.

The *communality* (h^2) of an observed variable is simply the square of the factor loadings for that variable (or the square of the correlation between that variable and the common factor), and the *uniqueness component* is simply $(1 - h^2)$.

The correlation between any two observed variables will be given by the multiplication of the two relevant factor loadings: $r_{ij} = (b_{iF})(b_{jF})$. This in turn implies that the residual correlation between X_i and X_j will be zero if the effect of the common factor is controlled: $r_{ij.F} = 0$.

Table 2 has been provided to illustrate the calculation of various coefficients, and to demonstrate the correspondence between theorems we have derived and the coefficients we actually calculated from the data. From this point on, we will assume that these theorems are self-evident and

TABLE 2
Illustration of Variance and Covariance:
Two-Variables, One-Common Factor

Source Variables			Observed Variables		Some Product Terms				
F	U_k	U_2	X_1	X_2	F^2	FU_1	FX_1	FX_2	X_1X_2
1	1	1	1.4	1.4	1	1	1.4	1.4	1.96
1	1	-1	1.4	-.2	1	1	1.4	-.2	-.28
1	-1	1	.2	1.4	1	-1	.2	1.4	.28
1	-1	-1	.2	-.2	1	-1	.2	-.2	-.04
-1	1	1	-.2	.2	1	-1	.2	-.2	-.04
-1	1	-1	-.2	-1.4	1	-1	.2	1.4	.28
-1	-1	1	-1.4	.2	1	1	1.4	-.2	-.28
-1	-1	-1	-1.4	-1.4	1	1	1.4	1.4	1.96
Sum					8	0	6.4	4.8	3.84
Expectation or Mean[a] =sum/N					1	0	0.8	0.6	0.48

a. The last row of numbers is equivalent, going from left to right, to var(F), cov(F,U_1), cov(F,X_2), cov(X_1,X_2).

Furthermore, since all the variables are standardized, all the covariances are equivalent to correlations.

apply them in more complex situations without deriving them every time.

Finally, you should observe that a one-common factor model does not imply that the variation in an observed variable is completely determined by the common factor; the unique component may actually be much larger than the communality. But observe that the *covariation* between the observed variables is *completely* determined by the common factor; if the common factor is removed, there will be no correlation between X_1 and X_2.

In summary, the distinguishing characteristic of the factor analytic approach is the assumption that observed covariation is due to some underlying common factors. Although we normally do not attempt to factor analyze a bivariate relationship (for reasons to be made clearer in later discussions), one actually is applying the factor analytic model by considering the correlation between two observed variables to be a result of their sharing of common sources or factors, and not as a result of one being a direct cause of the other.

Correspondence Between Factor Models and Covariance Structures

In a typical factor analysis situation, the researcher is given a matrix of covariances for a set of variables obtained from a sample. The researcher must then attempt to make two distinct types of inferences. The first involves making inferences about the factor structures (causal structures) underlying the observed covariance structure; the second type involves generalizing the first type of inference based on a given sample. The first type of inference is a logical one while the second is a statistical one. It is our belief that statistical problems are subsidiary to logical ones, especially when attempting to present the basic factor model.

In this section we will address the nature of the logical uncertainties inherent to factor analytic approaches; we will examine the correspondence between various properties of the factor model, such as number of common factors and lack of orthogonality among factors; and the properties of the covariance matrix, such as the rank of an adjusted covariance matrix. (Unless otherwise indicated, we will use the terms "covariance" and "correlation" synonymously.)

DERIVATION OF COVARIANCE STRUCTURE FROM THE FACTOR STRUCTURE

1. One-Common Factor with Many Variables: Extension of the results derived from the examination of Figure 1 to a situation where there are many observed variables is simple and straightforward. Figure 3 shows an example of one-common factor model with m observed variables.

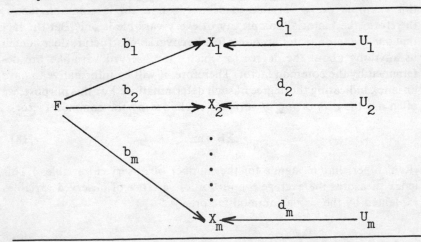

Figure 3: Path Model for a Multi-Variable, One-Common Factor Model

The diagram implies that cov(F, U_i) = 0, and cov(U_i, U_j) =0 and that the linear combinations involved are:

$$X_1 = b_1 F + d_1 U_1$$
$$X_2 = b_2 F + d_2 U_2$$
$$\cdots\cdots\cdots$$
$$X_m = b_m F + d_m U_m.$$

That is, we would arrive at the model shown in Figure 3 if we are given m + 1 source variables (F and Us) which are orthogonal to each other, and the m variables are created by linear operations. Since we assume that we know the factor model a priori, we have no problem in identifying b_1, b_2, ... b_m as factor loadings and b_1^2, b_2^2, ... b_m^2 as respective communalities. The correlations between the common factor and the variables are also equivalent to b_1, b_2, ... b_m, due to the assumptions that var(F) = var(U_i) = 1 and cov(F,U_i) and cov($U_i U_j$) = 0.

The resulting correlations between observed variables are from the theorems developed in Section II,

$$r_{12} = b_1 b_2, \; r_{13} = b_1 b_3 \ldots r_{1m} = b_1 b_m, \text{ and so on.}$$

Finally, the residual correlations between any two variables are zero— $r_{12.F} = r_{13.F} \ldots r_{1m.F} = 0$.

In describing the one common factor model, it is useful to introduce two additional concepts: *factorial complexity* of a variable and the degree of *factorial determination* of variables. The factorial complexity refers to the number of factors having (significant) loadings on a given variable. In this example every variable loads only on a single common factor, therefore, the factorial complexity of every variable is one. But the fact that one-common factor accounts for the covariance structure does not tell us anything about the degree to which the observed variables are determined by the common factor. Therefore, it will be informative to have an index indicating the degree of such determination. For this purpose, we often use the *proportion of variance* explained by the common factor,

$$\Sigma b_i^2 / m. \qquad [18]$$

(Remember that m stands for the number of observed variables.) This index measures the average proportion of variance of observed variables explained by the single common factor.

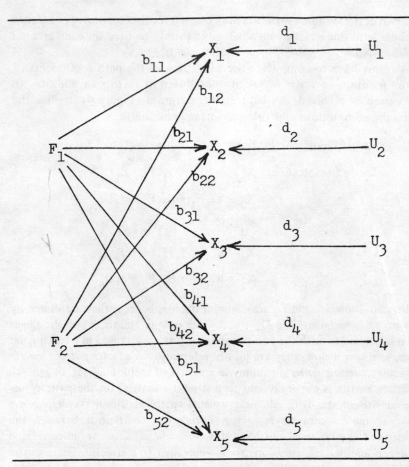

Figure 4: Path Model for Five-Variable, Two-Common Factor Model—The Orthogonal Case

2. *Two-Common Factors*: *The Orthogonal Case*: A one-common factor model, although useful in illustrating some of the basic properties, is too simple to demonstrate certain other properties of the factor model. We now describe a situation where the covariance in the observed variables is accounted for by two-common factors which are uncorrelated (orthogonal). We also use this opportunity to elaborate on more of the terminology encountered in factor analysis.

Now consider a situation in which you are given several source variables which are uncorrelated with each other. You are asked to create five variables by combining these sources variables linearly with the stipulation that two of these source variables may be used for the creation of every new variable, and one unique source variable should be used for each created variable (X_i).

We now have to complicate the subscripts of the path coefficients or factor loadings in order to specify the different factors in addition to the variables involved. As before, this diagram (Figure 4) implies the following assumptions and rules of linear combinations:

Assumptions: $\text{cov}(F_1, F_2) = \text{cov}(F_i, U_j) = \text{cov}(U_j U_k) = 0$.

Linear Combinations:
$$X_1 = b_{11}F_1 + b_{12}F_2 + d_1 U_1$$
$$X_2 = b_{21}F_1 + b_{22}F_2 + d_2 U_2$$
$$X_3 = b_{31}F_1 + b_{32}F_2 + d_3 U_3$$
$$X_4 = b_{41}F_1 + b_{42}F_2 + d_4 U_4$$
$$X_5 = b_{51}F_1 + b_{52}F_2 + d_5 U_5.$$

By definition, F_1 and F_2 are common factors because they are shared by two or more variables, and $U_1 \ldots U_5$ are unique factors. When the linear weights associated with the two-common factors are arranged in a rectangular form, as shown below, they are jointly referred to as a factor *pattern matrix* or factor *structure matrix,* or simply as a matrix of factor loadings. In general, a pattern matrix is not equivalent to a structure matrix, for the pattern matrix consists of standardized linear weights (path coefficients), whereas the structure matrix contains respective correlation coefficients between the factors and the observed variables. However, where factors are uncorrelated with one another, a pattern matrix is equivalent to a structure matrix. The fact that the correlation ($r_{F_j X_i}$) between a common factor (F_j) and a variable (X_i) is equivalent to the linear weight (b_{ij}) is derived from a simple extension of equations 11 through 14.

The decomposition of the variance of X_i is given by:

$$\text{var}(X_i) = b_{i1}^2 + b_{i2}^2 + d_i^2. \tag{19}$$

The proportion of variance of an observed variable (X_i) explained by the common factors—often referred to as the communality of variable i (h_i^2)—is given by:

$$h_i^2 = b_{i1}^2 + b_{i2}^2 \tag{20}$$

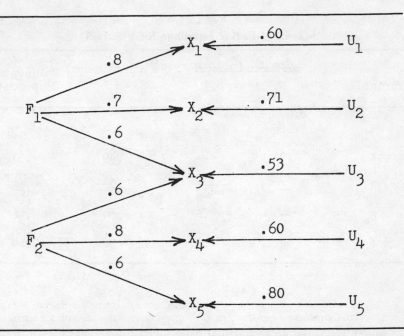

Figure 5: Path Model for Two-Common Factor Model Consistent with Data in Table 3

which is a simple extension of equations 8 through 10.

The covariance between any two observed variables (i and k) is likewise given by:

$$r_{ik} = b_{i1}b_{k1} + b_{i2}b_{k2} \qquad [21]$$

which is a simple extension of equations 15 and 16.

A specific example of a two factor model is presented in Figure 5. The matrix of factor loadings with appropriate statistics is presented in Table 3, following the usual format for reporting factor analytic results. The overall factorial determination is .570, indicating that 57 percent of the variance among the observed variables is determined by the two-common factors. The factor structure is very simple in that all the variables except X_3 have a factorial complexity of one. Of course, the factor loadings indicate both the causal weights as well as the correlations among given variables and factors.

The corresponding correlation matrix is presented in Table 4. Note the existence of zero correlations between the variables that do not share a common factor.

TABLE 3
Matrix of Factor Loadings for Figure 5

Variables	Common Factors			Uniqueness Component
	F_1	F_2	h_2	
X_1	.8	--	.64	.36
X_2	.7	--	.49	.51
X_3	.6	.6	.72	.28
X_4	--	.8	.64	.36
X_5	--	.6	.36	.64

3. *Two-Common Factors: The Oblique Case*: Now consider a situation in which five variables are created from seven source variables, as in the previous example, but with one additional complication. Two source variables are themselves correlated and these two are to be used as common factors. A general diagram depicting such a situation is presented in Figure 6.

TABLE 4
Correlation Matrix Corresponding to the
Factor Model Shown in Figure 5

	X_1	X_2	X_3	X_4	X_5
X_1	1.00	.56	.48	0	0
X_2		1.00	.56	0	0
X_3			1.00	.48	.36
X_4				1.00	.48
X_5					1.00

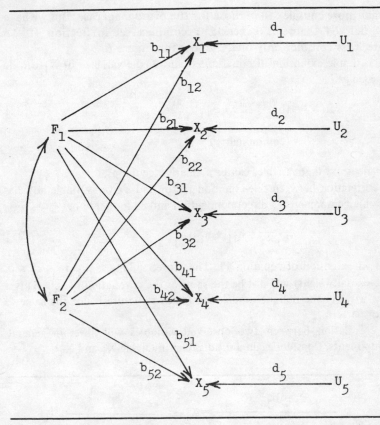

Figure 6: Path Model for a Five-Variable, Two Factor Model—The Oblique Case

The assumptions and rules of linear combinations for this model are the same as those for Figure 4, except that $\text{cov}(F_1, F_2) \neq 0$ in the oblique case. The rules for calculating the communalities and the various covariances are

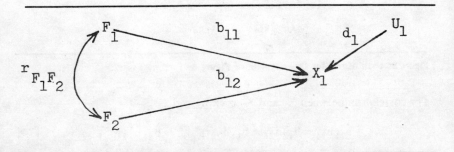

Figure 7: Path Model for One Segment of Figure 6

[30]

somewhat more complex than those for the orthogonal case. But we have already derived theorems covering a complex set in Section II. To illustrate, first consider only one segment for Figure 6.

By the simple extension of equations 8 and 9, the variance of X_1 can be decomposed as:

$$\text{var}(X_1) = (b_{11}^2 + b_{12}^2 + b_{11}b_{12}2r_{F_1F_2}) + d_1^2 \qquad [22]$$

$$= (\text{communality}) + d_1^2.$$

The variances of other variables can be similarly decomposed.

The correlation between one-common factor and a given variable now has two possible components—a direct connection and an indirect one:

$$r_{F_1X_1} = b_{11} + b_{12}r_{F_1F_2} \qquad [23]$$

which is an extension of equation 11. Therefore, as long as $(b_{12}r_{F_1F_2}) \neq 0$, b_{11} (the causal weight) will not be the same as the correlation $r_{F_1X_1}$. This is precisely why, in the oblique model, the factor structure is not the same as the factor pattern.

The correlation between two observed variables will have, in general, four components. Consider again a subdiagram involving X_1 and X_2:

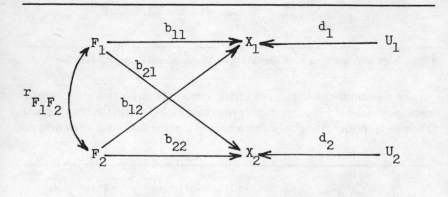

Figure 8: Path Model for One Segment of Figure 6

The correlation between X_1 and X_2 is expressed as:

$$r_{12} = b_{11}b_{21} + b_{12}b_{22} + b_{11}b_{22}r_{F_1F_2} + b_{21}b_{12}r_{F_1F_2} \qquad [24]$$

where the first component is due to the common sharing of F_1, the second component to the common sharing of F_2, the third and fourth components are due to the correlation between the factors. If $r_{F_1F_2} \neq 0$, equation 24 will be the same as equation 21. Equation 24 is also an extension of equation 11.

A concrete example of factorial causation that is exactly the same as Figure 5, except for the correlation between the common factors and adjustment of weights for the unique factors, is presented in Figure 9. (The adjustments in the weights for the unique factors are made to make the resulting variables have unit variances.)

In this case, the pattern matrix will have the same elements as the orthogonal case but the structure matrix will contain different elements. Table 5 presents all the necessary statistics.

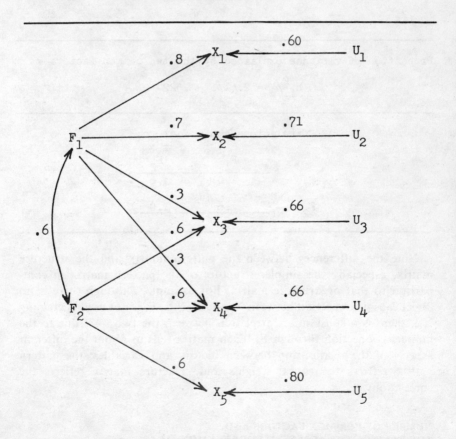

Figure 9: Path Model for an Oblique Two Factor Model Consistent with Data in Table 6

TABLE 5
An Oblique Two-Common Factor Model

Variables	Pattern Matrix			Structure Matrix	
	F_1	F_2	h_i^2	F_1	F_2
X_1	.8	--	.64	.80	.48
X_2	.7	--	.49	.70	.42
X_3	.3	.6	.56	.66	.78
X_4	.3	.6	.56	.66	.78
X_5	--	.6	.36	.36	.60

Proportion of variance explained by the two common factors =

$$h_i^2/_m = 2.61/_5 = .522$$

Correlations Among Factors

	F_1	F_2
F_1	1.0	.6
F_2	.6	1.0

Note the differences between the pattern matrix and the structure matrix, especially the simpler structure of the pattern matrix in comparison to that of structure matrix. For example, although there is no direct causal connection between X_1 and F_2 (i.e., F_2 is not used in creating X_1), there is a substantial correlation between the two (.48) due to the indirect connection through F_1. Each matrix tells us about the different aspects of the relationship between factors and variables: the pattern matrix reflects the causal weights and structure matrix reflects the correlations.

NUMBER OF COMMON FACTORS AND
THE RANK OF THE ADJUSTED CORRELATION MATRIX

In the preceding section we illustrated with several examples the principle that *if the factor structure is known*, the corresponding co-

TABLE 6
The Resulting Correlations and Communalities
Expressed in Terms of Factor Loadings,
Given A Common Factor Model

	X_1	X_2	X_3	X_4
X_1	b_1^2	$b_1 b_2$	$b_1 b_3$	$b_1 b_4$
X_2	$b_1 b_2$	b_2^2	$b_2 b_3$	$b_2 b_4$
X_3	$b_1 b_3$	$b_2 b_3$	b_3^2	$b_3 b_4$
X_4	$b_1 b_4$	$b_2 b_4$	$b_3 b_4$	b_4^2

a. The single subscripts are used because there is only one factor.

variance structure can be derived without error. In practice, however, one rarely (if ever) knows a priori what the factor structure is. Thus, it is necessary to begin to examine the more realistic situation of deriving underlying factors from the known relationships among the observed variables. As will be shown, however, the strategy of making inferences about factors from known correlations has associated with it a number of indeterminacies. These will be identified in this section. We will begin by examining another type of correspondence between the structural properties of factors and correlations. The structural property of concern is the relationship between the number of common factors and the independent dimensions of the resulting correlation matrix after certain adjustments have been made to it. Before proceeding, however, a cautionary note is necessary. This section may be difficult for some, especially those with limited backgrounds in mathematics. Hopefully, however, our interpretive remarks should be sufficient to convey the intent and meaning of this section.

We refer again to the one-common factor model as presented in Figure 3. Given the factor loadings, we can reproduce the correlations among the observed variables without error. In Table 6, these correlations are expressed in terms of the underlying factor loadings, and the diagonal entries are replaced by the communalities (this is possible given several of the basic theorems derived previously).

All adjusted correlation matrices (those with the communalities in the main diagonal) produced by one-common factor share a fundamental structural characteristic—the rank of the matrix is one. Without providing the formal mathematical basis and definitions, we will say that the rank of a matrix refers to the degree of linear dependence in a set of vectors forming the matrix. We believe it is necessary to briefly describe this concept and indicate how it is related to the notion of number of factors. One way to verify that a matrix has a rank of K is to find out if the determinants of the submatrices with K + 1 or more variables are all zeroes, and if there is at least one submatrix of dimension K whose determinant is not zero.

If the dimension or rank of the matrix is one, then all of the determinants involving two or more variables should be zero. This property may be illustrated by examining Table 6. For example, the determinant for the matrix involving the first two variables is:

$$\det \begin{pmatrix} b_1^2 & b_1 b_2 \\ b_1 b_2 & b_2^2 \end{pmatrix}$$

$$= b_1^2 b_2^2 - (b_1 b_2)(b_1 b_2)$$

(by definition of a determinant, which in the 2x2 matrix tells one to subtract the product of the elements in the secondary diagonal from the product of the elements in the main diagonal)

$$= b_1^2 b_2^2 - b_1^2 b_2^2 = 0 \qquad [25]$$

(by multiplying and subtracting).

By acknowledging that the main diagonal elements are communality estimates and that in the one-common factor case, the b's are the same as the corresponding correlations between variables and factors, we may write:

$$\det \begin{pmatrix} h_1^2 & r_{12} \\ r_{12} & h_2^2 \end{pmatrix} = 0. \qquad [26]$$

Likewise, every possible square matrix containing two or more rows and columns has a zero determinant.

For example:

$$\det \begin{pmatrix} r_{12} & r_{13} \\ b_2^2 & r_{23} \end{pmatrix} = \det \begin{pmatrix} b_1 b_2 & b_1 b_3 \\ b_2^2 & b_2 b_3 \end{pmatrix}. \qquad [27]$$

$$= (b_1 b_2)(b_2 b_3) - (b_1 b_3)(b_2^2) = 0.$$

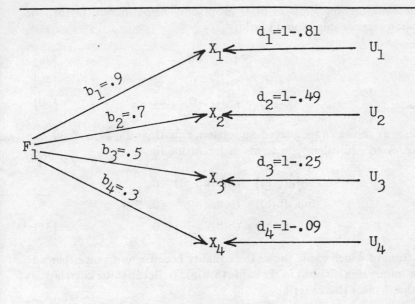

Figure 10: Path Model for Factor Model Consistent with Data in Table 7

As an empirical illustration, suppose that we are given a four variable correlation matrix which is based on the factor model depicted in Figure 10. The resulting correlation matrix without the main diagonal is presented in Table 7.

TABLE 7
Correlation Matrix Derived From the
Factor Model in Figure 10

	X_1	X_2	X_3	X_4
X_1	b_1^2	.63	.45	.27
X_2	.63	b_2^2	.35	.21
X_3	.45	.35	b_3^2	.15
X_4	.27	.21	.15	b_4^2

The rank-theorem implies that, given only one-common factor, the following relationships should hold:

$$r_{13}r_{24} - r_{14}r_{23} = 0 \qquad [28]$$

$$r_{12}r_{34} - r_{14}r_{23} = 0, \qquad [29]$$

$$r_{13}r_{24} - r_{12}r_{34} = 0, \qquad [30]$$

because, as shown in the preceding section, equations 28, 29, and 30, can be expressed equivalently in terms of factor loadings,

$$(b_1b_3)(b_2b_4) - (b_1b_4)(b_2b_3) = 0,$$
$$(b_1b_2)(b_3b_4) - (b_1b_4)(b_2b_3) = 0,$$
$$(b_1b_3)(b_2b_4) - (b_1b_2)(b_3b_4) = 0, \qquad [31]$$

inspection of which easily shows the equality because terms on either side of the minus sign amount to the same $(b_1b_2b_3b_4)$. Because the correlations in Table 7 meet this criterion,

$$(.45)(.21) - (.27)(.35) = 0,$$
$$(.63)(.15) - (.27)(.35) = 0,$$
$$(.45)(.21) - (.63)(.15) = 0,$$

we would confirm that one-common factor model fits the data.

Furthermore, continuing to use the theorem, we can ascertain the value of each communality and, therefore, the underlying factor loadings. For example, the rank-theorem also implies that

$$b_1{}^2r_{23} - r_{13}r_{12} = b_1{}^2r_{24} - r_{14}r_{12} - r_{14}r_{12} =$$
$$b_1{}^2r_{34} - r_{14}r_{13} = 0 \qquad [32]$$

which in turn implies that,

$$b_1{}^2 = r_{13}r_{12}/r_{23} = r_{14}r_{12}/r_{24} = r_{14}r_{13}/r_{34}. \qquad [33]$$

In our example,

$$b_1{}^2 = (.45)(.63)/.35 = (.27)(.63)/.21 = (.27)(.45)/.15 = .81.$$

The square root of .81 is .9 which agrees with the factor loading shown in Figure 10.

When there are two-common factors, the rank of the adjusted correlation matrix will be two, not one. At least one determinant involving two columns and rows will not be zero, but those for three or more columns and rows will always be zero. The formal proof for this has not been included. Most standard texts (e.g., Harman, Mulaik) provide such proofs. Those with knowledge of matrix algebra may benefit by deriving the results by calculating determinants for submatrices of various dimensions. Those who have had some exposure to the discussion of multicolinearity in regression, may think of the rank problem in terms of complete determination in multiple regression—if the rank of the adjusted correlation matrix is one, it means that all the entries in one column can be predicted by the entries of another (without error); if the rank is two, the entries in any column can be determined completely by the linear combination of entries in any other two columns, and so on. Keep in mind, however, that we are evaluating the entries in a correlation matrix, and not the values in a standard data matrix.

To sum up, what we have attempted to demonstrate thus far with this discussion of matrices, ranks, determinants, and so on, is a basic principle about the correspondence between the number of common factors and the rank of the adjusted correlation matrix. The principle is: if the number of factors is known to be K, one may infer that the rank of the corresponding adjusted correlation matrix also is K. Such a correspondence suggests that the reverse of this inferential process is possible, that is, that the number of underlying common factors can be ascertained *from examination of the adjusted correlation matrix.* It was, in fact, the examination of such a correspondence that made factor analysis possible, at least, in its early development. As will be shown, however, inferences of this type are not as straightforward and unequivocal as when the factor structure is known. In particular, use of the rank theorem is restricted because of the following complications: (1) when there are two or more common factors, the exact configuration of loadings cannot be ascertained without additional assumptions; (2) the rank-theorem applies only when the causal operations (the rules for combining factors to create variables) meet a certain set of conditions; (3) the observed correlations are contaminated by the sampling and measurement errors; (4) the relationships in the real world even without sampling and measurement errors may not fit any factor model exactly.

Sampling and measurement problems will be addressed in a separate section, where various statistical issues are discussed. The remaining three problems are conceptual ones, arising from the inherent uncertainties in the relationship between the factor structure and covariance structure. Before the strategies of handling these problems are discussed, we will illustrate the main sources of these problems.

UNCERTAINTIES INHERENT TO
DERIVING FACTORS FROM COVARIANCE STRUCTURES

The properties of linear causal systems are simple and straightforward. Moreover, there is an unequivocal covariance structure associated with every linear causal system. That is, if the factor loadings are known, then correlations among the variables may be uniquely derived. But as already alluded to, the converse is not necessarily true. Knowledge of correlations among the observed variables does not lead to knowledge of the underlying causal structure, because the same covariance structure can be produced by many different causal structures. Thus, the main objective of factor analysis—to ascertain the underlying factorial structure from the examination of a covariance structure—is not as easily accomplished.

It is quite possible, however, that we may be able to eliminate the uncertainties to some extent if their nature is well understood. There are three basic types of problems which result in uncertainties about the relationship between the underlying causal structure and the resulting covariance structure: (1) a particular covariance structure can be produced by the same number of common factors but with a *different configuration* of factor loadings; (2) a particular covariance structure can be produced by factor models with *different numbers* of common factors; (3) a particular covariance structure can be produced by a factor analytic causal model as well as a non-factor analytic causal model. Before discussing implications of these three sources of uncertainty, some concrete examples of each type are presented.

(1) *One Covariance Structure—Different Factor Loadings:* There are two versions of this type of uncertainty. Both of the causal structures in Figure 11 have two orthogonal factors but the factor loadings are different. Nevertheless, the resulting correlation matrices among the observed variables are identical except for rounding errors.

In general, there is an infinite number of such different configurations which can lead to the same correlation matrix. Therefore, determining the configuration of the linear weights actually operating in reality by examining the correlations among the observed variables is nothing more than guesswork (assuming no theory or past research findings).

A second example is illustrated in Figure 12 where one causal system is based on oblique factors while the other is based on orthogonal ones. Both produce the same correlation matrix for the observed variables.

In factor analytic literature, the type of uncertainty being illustrated here is often called the *problem of rotation*. The problems of rotation are dealt with in the companion volume.

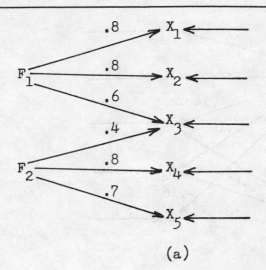

(a)

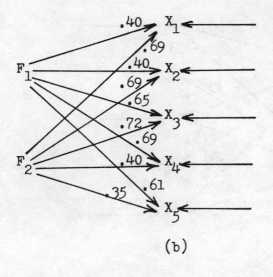

(b)

Figure 11: Path Models for Factor Models Consistent with a Single Correlation Matrix

(2) *One Covariance Structure—Varying Number of Factors:* When discussing the correspondence between the number of common factors and the rank of the adjusted correlation matrix of variables, we did not fully specify the conditions under which this correspondence exists. Figure

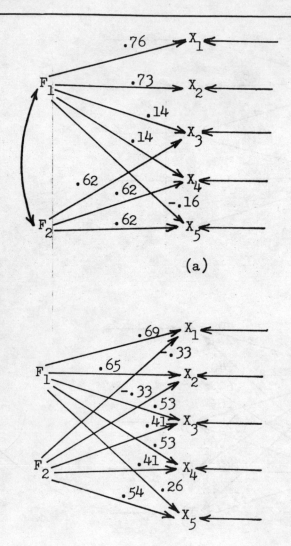

(a)

(b)

Figure 12: Path Models for Factor Models Consistent with a Single Correlation Matrix

13 shows two causal structures both leading to the same correlation matrix.

The important point to remember from this illustration is that one cannot infer the number of common factors responsible for the given

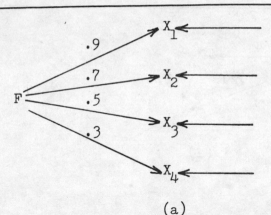

(a)

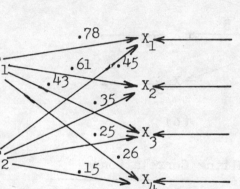

(b)

Figure 13: Path Models for Factor Models Consistent with a Single Correlation Matrix

correlation matrix; models with a greater number of common factors could have produced the same type of correlation matrix. It will be shown later that this uncertainty can be considered a special case of the general problem of *rotation*.

(3) *Competing Causal Structures:* Another fundamental uncertainty is that a variety of different causal relationships can lead to the same correlation structure. We mentioned at the beginning of Section II that the factor analytic approach typically assumes that the correlation be-

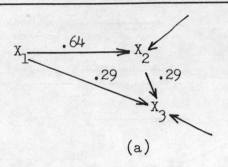

(a)

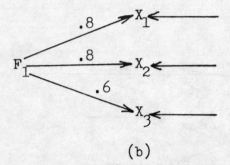

(b)

Resulting Correlations

	X_1	X_2	X_3
X_1	--	.64	.48
X_2		--	.48
X_3			--

Figure 14: Path Models Representing Two Causal Structures Which Result in the Same Correlations

tween two variables is due to their sharing of common factors. The correlation between two variables, X_1 and X_2, can be produced in several ways: (1) X_1 being the cause of X_2, (2) X_1 and X_2 sharing some common causes, or (3) by the combination of both.

Figure 14 gives two causal structures with three variables each, which result in the same correlational structure. One is a one-common factor model and the other is not a factor model.

The critical question then becomes whether it is possible to test empirically with the data whether the factor model is appropriate for the data. The answer is a simple "no." This type of indeterminacy is solved only by an imposition of the factor analytic structure purely on the basis of a theoretical argument, or the knowledge of the causal ordering among the variables based on previous research.

In a sense, problem 3 above is more serious than 2, and problem 2 is more serious than 1, because 3 implies that appropriateness of the factor analytic interpretation can never be proved, problem 2 implies that the number of common factors can never be proved, and 1 implies only that factor loadings may be different. These dilemmas may be resolved only by making assumptions.

Fundamental Postulates of Factor Analysis: Recapitulation

In the face of these seemingly insurmountable uncertainties inherent in examining the relationship between factorial structure and covariance structure, how does one apply factor analysis and have any assurance that the findings can be interpreted meaningfully? As with most other scientific methods, we try to minimize these uncertainties by relying on certain postulates. We use the term postulate to refer to basic assumptions or principles which must be adhered to by the users of factor analysis if the uncertainties are to be minimized. Some postulates may be more appropriate than the others for a given problem, but their ultimate validity is always subject to doubt.

The assumption one has to make even before attempting to use factor analysis may be called the *postulate of factorial causation*. Given relationships among variables, this postulate imposes a particular causal order on the data—that observed variables are linear combinations of some underlying causal variables. The researcher has to substantiate this postulate on the basis of other substantive knowledge about the data; the results of applying the factor analytic technique cannot be used to substantiate the validity of the postulate. The most that can be achieved is the conclusion that the structure of the observed data is not inconsistent with a particular factor model based on such a postulate. In other words, given these variables and covariation among them, it is the burden of the researcher to argue that the underlying causal structure is factorial as in Figure 14b instead of some other as in Figure 14a.

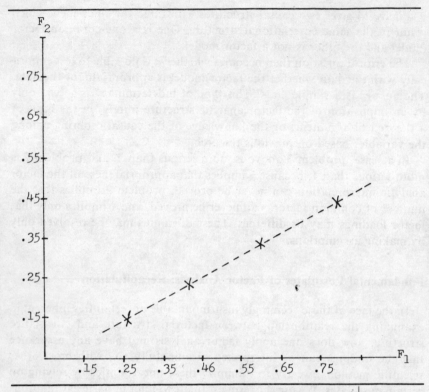

Figure 15: Cartesian Coordinate System for Factor Model in Figure 13a

The second indeterminacy (one-covariance structure—varying number of factors) is resolved by adopting the *postulate of parsimony*. For example, given that both one-common factor and two-common factor models are consistent with the observed data, we accept on faith the more parsimonious model. Thus, given the two postulated models shown in Figure 13, we would choose (a) over (b). Such an assumption is not provable but is widely accepted in other fields of research.

One technical advantage of accepting this principle is that it often leads to a unique conclusion where such a conclusion is impossible otherwise. Again going back to Figure 13, there are infinite numbers of factor models that might have produced the observed correlation matrix, but there is only one particular configuration of factor loadings that is consistent with the one-common factor model. Here the rank-theorem on the correspondence between the number of common factors and the number of dimensions of the adjusted correlation matrix can be a useful tool. The hypothesis of interest is that there is a single common factor, which is the objective given the principle of parsimony. Application of the rank-theorem will alow one to "reject" or "not reject" this hypothesis. But failing to reject it does not prove that a single common factor accounts for the covariation among the variables. Stated another way, it is possible to determine if the data are consistent or inconsistent with a one-common factor model, but given that consistency is indicated, it is impossible to prove there is only one factor.

A reexamination of the two models in Figure 13 is informative at this point. In Figure 15 we represent the factor loadings of Figure 13b on a Cartesian coordinate system.

It is immediately clear that all these loadings line up on the dotted line. If we were to use the dotted line (which is 30 degrees from F_1 counter clockwise) as the new coordinate system, we will find the loadings on this new axis will be equivalent to the loadings shown in Figure 13a. In this sense, the *postulate of parsimony* is related to *rotation* (or data transformation) which is used more frequently in order to find a more "meaningful" or "interpretable" factorial structure.

As already indicated, the first indeterminacy (one covariance structure—different factor loadings) is often called the *problem of rotation*. Here the number of common factors is no longer an issue. A certain degree of parsimony is achieved by selecting the minimum number of common factors which could produce the observed covariance structure. But the question is how to choose between (a) and (b) of Figures 11 and 12.

Given the particular factor patterns in these models, it is relatively easy to argue that the "a" models display a greater degree of simplicity than their "b" counterparts in that some variables in the "a" models have factorial complexity of one, while all the variables in "b" have factorial complexity of two.

In actual factor analysis, where one has to deal with sampling and measurement errors, the choice may never be clear-cut. The final choice may be a matter of personal preference, because the appropriate rotation of axes (allowing obliqueness) can change one system to another without affecting the degree of fit between any of the rotated factorial systems and the given covariance structure. This is why the general problem of rotation is separated from the rotation leading to minimum factors. The latter is accepted as a fundamental guiding principle, but the former has not achieved such a general acceptance. A "simpler structure" for one researcher may not be a "simpler structure" for the other. The problem of rotation is covered in greater detail in University Paper 07-014, *Factor Analysis: Statistical Methods and Practical Issues.*

In summary, the factor analytic approach is possible only when the postulates of factorial causation and parsimony are accepted. We have illustrated why these postulates are necessary by showing the inherent indeterminacies in making inferences about the underlying causal struc-

[46]

tures from the observation of the covariance structure for the observed variables. These indeterminacies are logical, not statistical, in nature. We will treat factor analysis as a statistical tool and discuss its many variants in University Paper 07-014.

III. OBTAINING FACTOR ANALYSIS SOLUTIONS

In the remainder of this volume, we will describe the basic steps in doing factor analysis through the use of existing computer packages. It is our belief that it is essential that potential users be introduced to actual applications right from the beginning so they can relate more meaningfully to the varieties and complexities of actual factor analysis.

Major Steps in Actual Factor Analysis

In the preceding section, we examined the relationships between factors and variables assuming that the factor structure is known and that there are no measurement or sampling errors. We have identified basic uncertainties inherent in the process of making inferences about the underlying factor structure from the examination of covariance structures. We noted that these uncertainties are reduced only with the introduction of the postulates of factorial causation and parsimony. To be realistic, however, we must consider how these postulates are applied to the analysis of actual data which are subject to sampling and measurement errors. In this situation not only must one make inferences about the factorial structure from the examination of the covariance structure, but also make inferences about the population values from the examination of the sample statistics. Although this introduces a number of complexities, there are standard procedures for dealing with them. These are discussed fully in the companion volume, *Factor Analysis: Statistical Methods and Practical Issues*.

In this section we will provide an introduction to and illustration of how to obtain factor solutions by using existing packaged computer programs. This will provide enough information to allow a potential user to actually do factor analysis. Prior to presenting this, however, it is necessary to describe the major steps in applying exploratory factor analysis to actual data. There are four basic steps: (1) the data collection and preparation of the relevant covariance matrix, (2) the extraction of the initial factors, (3) the rotation to a terminal solution and interpretation, (4) construction of factor scales and their use in further analysis. Our discussion of each of these steps assumes that the reader will rely on computers for the data handling and analysis.

TABLE 8
Example of a Data Matrix

Entity	Variables			
	1	2	3	m
1	5	20	9	52
2	3	18	10	48
3	2	31	11	21
4	1	15	8	63
.				.
.				.
.				.
.				.
.				.
.				.
i	9	22	14	21

DATA COLLECTION AND PREPARATION
OF THE COVARIANCE MATRIX

The first step in factor analysis is collecting the relevant data for analysis and, as mentioned in the preceding sections, preparing a covariance matrix, the data used directly in the factor analysis. Many times the co-variance matrix is already available, but if not, the first step involves collecting information on a set of entities or objects for the variables of interest. For example, if one is interested in factor analyzing political attitudes of citizens, the objects (in this case, a given number of citizens) must be sampled and surveyed through interviews or other means regarding their views on various political issues. These basic data must then be arranged in a systematic way, usually called a data matrix. An example of such a matrix is given in Table 8.

Note that the data matrix has two modes (or dimensions): (1) the *entity mode* representing the objects or cases, which in the example is citizens, arranged as rows, and (2) the *variable mode* represented by different columns. The covariance matrix desired in ordinary factor analysis is for the relationships among variables (columns). We should mention in passing, however, that it also is possible to examine the "similarities" between objects (between rows) as defined in terms of their total profile on these variables. (See literature on cluster analysis and Q-factor analysis: Tryon and Bailey, 1970; Stephenson, 1953). Furthermore, it is possible to expand the data matrix by asking the same questions on the same subjects on different occasions. Then the data would contain three modes, not two, and such data can be analyzed by using three-mode factor analysis (See Tucker, 1966). But almost all factor analyses reported in the research literature deal with data in the basic two modes as shown in Table 8, and thus, our discussion is only in terms of this type.

Assuming that the basic covariance structure (matrix) of interest is for the variables, one could still make the choice between analyzing the *covariance* matrix or the *correlation* matrix. Because this issue requires a fairly lengthy discussion, we have delayed its presentation to our companion volume. Here we suggest that in exploratory factor analysis, one may rely on the use of a correlation matrix. Two practical advantages make this choice advisable: (1) many existing computer programs do not accept the covariance matrix as basic input data, and (2) almost all of the examples in the literature are based on correlation matrices—hence it will be easier for the reader to understand and compare results with others.

EXTRACTING INITIAL FACTORS

The second major step in factor analysis is to find the number of factors that can adequately explain the observed correlations (or covariances) among the observed variables. The typical approach at this stage is to input the relevant matrix into a factor analysis program and choose one of the many methods of obtaining the initial solution. There are several major alternatives: (1) maximum likelihood method (or canonical factoring), (2) least-squares method (variants are principal axis factoring with iterated communalities or Minres), (3) Alpha factoring, (4) Image factoring, and (5) principal components analysis. These alternatives are discussed in detail in the companion volume. Our advice is, that until a more complete understanding of the methods is gained, the researcher should use one of the first two methods, or the default option in the program.

At this stage of the analysis one should not be concerned with whether the underlying factors are orthogonal or oblique—all the initial solutions are based on the orthogonal solution. Nor should one be too concerned with whether the factors extracted are interpretable or meaningful. The chief concern is whether a smaller number of factors can account for the covariation among a much larger number of variables.

It also should be mentioned at this point that to obtain an initial solution the researcher must provide (1) either the number of common factors to be extracted, or (2) the criterion by which such a number can be determined. The reader should recall the rank-theorem in factor analysis which states that, in error-free data, the rank of the adjusted correlation matrix produced by k common factors is k. However, there are two reasons why this theorem is not used directly in factor analysis. First, the observed data are subject to many random errors, or, at the least, to sampling error, and therefore, an exact fit between the data and the model cannot be expected. Second, related to this first problem is the fact that one cannot ascertain the exact communalities.

The most commonly used procedure of determining the number of initial factors to be extracted is a rule-of-thumb—the rule known either as the Kaiser or eigenvalue criterion (eigenvalue greater than or equal to 1). Then the corresponding communalities are estimated iteratively, usually starting with some initial values (either specified by the researcher or more commonly in packaged programs, given by the multiple R-squared value between a given variable and the other variables) and ending with values to which successive reestimates or refinements converge. Some of the methods, such as the maximum likelihood solution, also provide large-sample statistical significance tests by which the adequacy of the initial guess (or the rule-of-thumb) can be evaluated. Several alternative means of determining the number of factors are more fully discussed in the companion volume. Until these are learned, we recommend that the user rely on the default options available with the particular computer program in use.

ROTATION TO A TERMINAL SOLUTION

To obtain the *initial* solution, certain restrictions typically are imposed. These restrictions are (1) there are k common factors, (2) underlying factors are orthogonal to each other, and (3) the first factor accounts for as much variance as possible, the second factor accounts for as much of the residual variance left unexplained by the first factor, the third factor accounts for as much of the residual variance left unexplained by the first two factors, and so on. The first restriction remains in effect throughout a given factor analysis, although its adequacy can be partially tested in certain methods of initial factoring and can be modified in subsequent factor analyses. The second and third restrictions are considered arbitrary, and one or both are removed in the rotation stage in order to obtain simpler and more readily interpretable results.

We remind the reader that no method of rotation improves the degree of fit between the data and the factor structure. Any rotated factor solution explains exactly as much covariation in the data as the initial solution. What is attempted through rotation is a possible "simplification." There exist different criteria of simplicity which lead to different methods of rotation. These various criteria of "simple structure" are discussed in the companion volume.

Our advice to the user is that one should not be unduly concerned about the choice of the particular rotation method. If identification of the basic structuring of variables into theoretically meaningful subdimensions is the primary concern of the researcher, as is often the case in an exploratory factor analysis, almost any readily available method of rotation will do the job. Even the issue of whether factors are correlated or not may not make much difference in the exploratory stages of analysis. It even can be argued that employing a method of orthogonal rotation (or maintaining the arbitrary imposition that the factors remain orthogonal) may be preferred over oblique rotation, if for no other reason than that the former is much simpler to understand and interpret. Nevertheless, the distinction between orghogonal and oblique rotations is important for a fuller understanding of the factor structure. We advise that beginners choose one of the commonly available methods of rotation, such as Varimax if orthogonal rotation is sought or Direct Oblimin if oblique rotation is sought. As the reader's understanding of factor analysis deepens, by becoming more acquainted with basic results of factor analysis, the variety of proposed criteria may be studied and "experimented" with.

CONSTRUCTION OF FACTOR SCALES
AND THEIR USE IN FURTHER ANALYSIS

With the exceptions of psychology and education, it is not misleading to argue that the main motivation behind the use of factor analysis is not in ascertaining the factor structure among a set of variables, but in achieving data reduction and obtaining factor scales which can be used as variables in a different study. Today it is not unusual to see factor scales being analyzed along with other variables, with no more fanfare than a brief note somewhere indicating that some of the variables are factor scales obtained through factor analysis.

Most factor analysis computer programs usually produce coefficients (or weights) with which to combine the observed variables to represent the underlying factor, and some even create such scales for the user. Therefore, creating factor scales from factor analysis is not a difficult task. But the user must be warned that factor scales so created, whichever method may have been selected, are not the same as the underlying factors. Not only are the correlations between the hypothetical factor and the corresponding scale likely to be much less than 1.0, but also the relationships among the scales are not likely to be the same as the relationships among the underlying factors. What we are emphasizing is that one should not forget the fact that factor scales are error-prone indicators of the underlying factors.

A more detailed discussion of various methods of constructing factor scales will appear in the companion volume. Here we merely note that factor scales for the underlying factors constructed by using different methods ȷusually correlate very highly with each other—in contrast to the fact that a given scale may not correlate as highly with the underlying hypothetical factor. This may relieve the anxiety on the part of the user who must choose one out of many options for constructing factor scales, or who may not have a choice and must rely on what is built into the program being used. It should also be noted that some analysis methods such as covariance-structure analysis and confirmatory factor analysis can handle both hypothetical variables such as factors and "raw" variables in the same analysis, which mitigates the need to rely on constructing "inadequate" factor scales. This point will be discussed more fully in the companion volume.

Illustration of Actual Analysis, as Applied to Known Error-Free Data

These major steps will be illustrated by applying factor analysis to a data set whose underlying factor structure is known, and where the observed data are free from sampling and measurement errors. We will then complicate the picture by introducing sampling and other practical problems.

For heuristic purposes suppose we know the underlying factor structure for a given set of variables. Let us consider a model that is somewhat more complex than the models examined in Section II, and thus a little more realistic. In particular, suppose there are two correlated factors underlying citizens' political attitudes, with a causal pattern as shown in Figure 16.

The first factor, F_1, is responsible for the covariation among the first three variables dealing with economic issues; the second factor, F_2, is responsible for the covariation among civil rights issues. There are also correlations between the first three and the last three variables because of the correlation between the two factors.

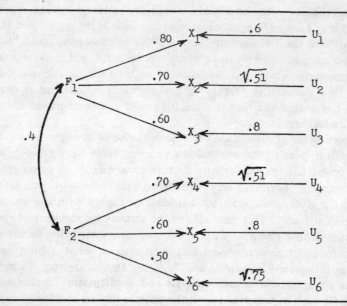

Figure 16: Path Model for Six-Variable, Two Oblique Factor Model Example, where the observed variables represent opinions on:

X_1 = whether government should spend more money on schools,
X_2 = whether government should spend more money to reduce unemployment,
X_3 = whether government should control big business,
X_4 = whether government should expedite desegregation, through busing,
X_5 = whether government sees to it that minorities get their respective quota in jobs,
X_6 = whether government should expand the headstart program.

In the population, such a factor pattern will produce a correlation matrix shown in Table 9. From Section II, it should be obvious that the basic data for factor analysis are a matrix of such correlations or co-variances. (Unless otherwise noted, we will treat correlations and co-variances as equivalent because we assume throughout most of our discussion that all the variables are standardized.)

Given such a matrix of correlations, one may directly proceed to examine the patterns of correlations and apply factor analysis. For example, we notice that there are two sets of clusters; the correlations among the first three variables and among the last three variables are in general higher than correlations between them, alerting the researcher to the possibility of finding two factors. However, in actual exploratory factor analysis the researcher may not have noticed such a patterning; it is fairly obvious in our example only because we have arranged the variables in a particular order.

TABLE 9
Correlation Matrix for Political Opinion Variables

	X_1	X_2	X_3	X_4	X_5	X_6
X_1	1.000	.560	.480	.224	.192	.160
X_2	.560	1.000	.420	.196	.168	.140
X_3	.480	.420	1.000	.168	.144	.120
X_4	.224	.196	.168	1.000	.420	.350
X_5	.192	.168	.144	.420	1.000	.300
X_6	.160	.140	.120	.350	.300	1.000

a. Variables are identified in Figure 16.

Suppose we decide to do an exploratory factor analysis for this correlation matrix and use some existing packaged computer program. Also, suppose we decide on the maximum likelihood solution, and, being a novice to factor analysis, simply do not know how many factors to extract and, therefore, decide to start with a one-common factor model.

The maximum likelihood solution finds the most likely population values that would have produced the given correlation matrix under the hypothesis (in this case) that a one-common factor model fits the data perfectly in the population and the joint distribution is multivariate normal. In this particular case, the hypothesis is wrong; we know that the correlation matrix is created by a two-common factor model. Nevertheless, it is heuristically useful to see what happens when we specify a smaller number of factors than there really are. Table 10 presents the major statistics produced by the solution (on the assumption that the sample size was 100).

The maximum likelihood solutions provide the pattern matrix (the loadings) and the estimated communalities, and a few additional statistics with which to evaluate the adequacy of the solution. In a one-common factor model communalities are no more than the squares of the respective factor loadings, and the total amount of variance explained is given by the sum of communalities. The most important question at this stage of initial factoring is whether or not the given factors adequately account for the observed correlations among the variables.

TABLE 10
**Results of Fitting A One-Common Factor Model
to the Political Opinion Data in Table 9:
Maximum Likelihood Solution**

Variables	F_1	Communalities	Communalities Implied by the Model
X_1	.774	.5995	.64
X_2	.696	.4842	.49
X_3	.598	.3573	.36
X_4	.345	.1193	.49
X_5	.306	.0939	.36
X_6	.263	.0690	.25

Amount of Variance Explained = 1.723

Percentage of Variance Explained = $(1.723/6)100 = 28.7$

χ^2- statistic with 9 degrees of freedom = 26.4

The expected correlations given the factor loadings in Table 10 are $r_{12} = (.774)(.696) = .5387$, $r_{13} = (.774)(.598) = .4529$, $r_{14} = (.774)(.345) = .2670$, and so on. The fit is not exact and there is substantial discrepancy when the relationships among the last three variables are considered (compare with Table 9). Since we know the true model that produced the observed correlations, we can also compare the estimated communalities with true communalities. We again notice (by comparing the last two columns of Table 10) that the discrepancy is substantial with respect to the last three variables. In real analysis, however, one does not know the true values and must rely on some other criterion, such as examining the fit between the observed correlations and those produced by a given factor model. The particular method we have selected provides an approximate large-sample χ^2-test to evaluate whether the data deviate significantly from the model, and in this case the deviation is statistically significant. We would, therefore, reject the adequacy of one-common factor model.

Having rejected the one-common factor model, it is logical to test the compatibility of a two-common factor model with the data. A solution (based on maximum likelihood procedures) is given in Table 11.

TABLE 11
Unrotated Factor Loadings (Pattern) for the
Maximum Likelihood Canonical Solution:
Political Opinion Example

Vars$_{(i)}$	Factors		Communalities
	F_1	F_2	
	b_{i1}	b_{i2}	
X_1	.766	-.232	.640
X_2	.670	-.203	.490
X_3	.574	-.174	.360
X_4	.454	.533	.490
X_5	.389	.457	.360
X_6	.324	.381	.250
Eigenvalues	1.827	.763	Sum = 2
Percent of Variance Explained	30.5	12.7	
Cumulative Percent of Variance Explained	30.5	43.2	

$\chi^2 = 0.$

We may check whether a two-common factor model is compatible with the data by comparing correlations with those expected, assuming the two-common factor model to be correct. The expected correlations (r_{ij}) due to the two hypothesized factors are given by

$$r_{ij} = b_{i1}b_{j1} + b_{i2}b_{j2}. \qquad [34]$$

For example, the expected correlation between X_1 and X_2 is

$$r_{12} = b_{11}b_{21} + b_{12}b_{22} = (.766)(.670) + (-.232)(-.203) = .56,$$

which is the observed correlation. Likewise, every other expected correlation (not presented here) is the same as the corresponding observed correlation. In addition, the χ^2- statistic indicates the adequacy of the model. Hence, we would accept that a two-common factor model is compatible with the observed correlation matrix. So far, then, we have accomplished what is usually known as the initial solution or initial extraction of factors.

We should note that the same result would have been obtained in a single step if we had specified from the beginning the criterion that the number of initial factors be equal to the number of roots (eigenvalues) of the matrix that are greater than 1.0, or if we had set the limit of the maximum number of factors to be extracted at two (perhaps based on knowledge gained by examining the patterning of coefficients in the correlation matrix).

Before we consider the second major step, it is useful to comment on how the factor pattern given in Table 11 might be interpreted. The nonzero loadings on the first factor indicate that every variable in the set shares something in common. We might, therefore, call this first factor a general liberalism factor. It indicates that if a person holds a liberal opinion on one item that same person tends to hold a liberal opinion on another. This first factor might also be called a general conservatism factor or even a liberalism-conservatism factor. It is important to emphasize, however, that factor analysis does not tell the researcher what substantive labels or meaning to attach to the factors. This decision must be made by the researcher. Factor analysis is purely a statistical technique indicating which, and to what degree, variables relate to an underlying and undefined factor. The substantive meaning given to a factor is typically based on the researcher's careful examination of what the high loading variables measure. Put another way, the researcher must ask what these variables have in common. As will be discussed, certain factor solutions make this task easier.

Our examination of the factor pattern would also tell us that the second factor is bi-polar, i.e., it loads positively on some variables and negatively on others. Although such a bi-polar pattern indicates that there are two sets of variables which tap somewhat distinct dimensions, the interpretation of the bi-polar factor is not readily apparent; that is, we do not know what to call it. It is possible, however, to define this second factor with respect to the first; among those cases with a similar degree of overall liberalism (the same value on factor 1), those who have liberal opinions on the one set of variables tend to have conservative opinions on the other set. We must admit that such an interpretation is more complex than desirable, and we still want a factor solution that makes interpretation easier. (We remind the reader that in this case the model shown in Figure 16 is the true model, but in actual data analysis we would not have access to such information.)

Having found the minimum number of factors that can account for the observed correlations, the next step is to rotate the axis to get a simpler and/or more easily interpretable solution. At this stage, the researcher again has to make a few decisions: whether to use an orthogonal rotation (i.e., to assume that factors are uncorrelated), or an oblique rotation (i.e., to assume that factors may be correlated). In addition, one will have to choose which particular method to use. For heuristic purposes we will examine both an orthogonal rotation based on the Varimax criterion and an oblique solution, known as Direct Oblimin.

Before resorting to computer programs for rotation, let us examine a graphic presentation of the unrotated factor solution. Remember from Section II that it is possible to use a cartesian coordinate system to repre-

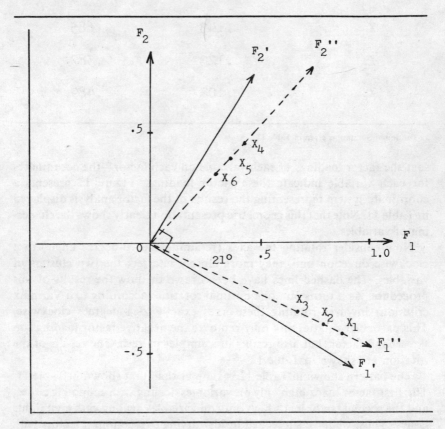

Figure 17: Factor Pattern Matrix for Table 11

Key:
F_1 and F_2: orthogonal factors (axes) before rotation;
F_1' and F_2': orthogonal factors after Varimax rotation;
F_1'' and F_2'': oblique factors after Direct Oblimin rotation. The angle between the two is 66.42°.

TABLE 12
Varimax Rotated Factor Pattern:
Political Opinion Example

Variables	F_1	F_2
X_1	.783	.163
X_2	.685	.143
X_3	.587	.123
X_4	.143	.685
X_5	.123	.587
X_6	.102	.489

a. The Initial Solution is given in Table 11.

sent the factor loadings of each variable on each factor—the coordinates for each variable indicate these factor loadings. Figure 17 presents a coordinate system representing the results of the factor analysis displayed in Table 11. Note that this geometric presentation clearly shows the clustering of variables.

Now consider rotating the axes (retaining the 90-degree angle) in a clockwise direction until they more closely intersect the two clusters of variables. The dashed lines have been drawn to show the results of this procedure. As it turns out, one optimal rotation (according to a Varimax criterion) involves rotating these axes exactly 29.1 degrees clockwise. This particular rotation not only removes the negative factor loadings on the second factor, but also results in a simpler pattern. The results of the rotation are shown in Table 12.

The pattern shown in Table 12 is simpler than that shown in Table 11. The first factor loads high only on variables dealing with economic issues, and the second factor loads high only on variables dealing with civil rights issues. Thus, we have succeeded in identifying two common factors with a relatively clear pattern; there is apparently one factor (an economic dimension) that is responsible for correlations among the first three variables, and another factor (a civil rights dimension) that is responsible for correlations among the last three variables.

TABLE 13
Factor Pattern and Factor Structure After Oblique
Rotation: Political Opinion Example

Variables	Pattern Matrix F_1	F_2	Structure Matrix F_1	F_2
X_1	.800	.000	.800	.320
X_2	.700	.000	.700	.280
X_3	.600	.000	.600	.240
X_4	.000	.700	.280	.700
X_5	.000	.600	.240	.600
X_6	.000	.500	.200	.500

a. The pattern matrix is an exact replica of loadings shown in Figure 16. The structure matrix shows the correlations between the factors and variables.

One could proceed further, however. A closer inspection of Figure 17 also shows that the clustering of two groups of variables forms an oblique angle (i.e., if the axes are placed directly through the two clusters, they no longer are at right angles). We should explore the possibility of an even simpler pattern by rotating each axis individually and, thereby, letting the two axes form an oblique angle. The result of applying an oblique rotation is given in Table 13, and the rotated axes are drawn in Figure 17. In a sense, the loadings in Table 13 are simpler than the loadings in Table 11, but at the "expense" of incorporating correlations between the two factors. In this case, the choice between the orthogonal and oblique factor models is relatively clear-cut, but it may not always be as clear in practice. Ultimately, one will have to make such a decision based on some theoretical expectations and extrastatistical knowledge about the nature of the data.

Let us recapitulate the steps we have followed in illustrating the application of factor analysis to error-free data. First, we selected a set of variables and prepared a matrix of correlation coefficients. Second, we tried to determine the minimum number of common factors that could have produced the observed correlations. Third, through rotation, we settled on the simplest solution among a potentially infinite number of solutions that are equally compatible with the observed correlations. We are now ready to address a few important issues the user confronts when dealing with actual data.

Obtaining Basic Factor Analysis Solutions
Through the Use of Computer Packages

When learning a complex subject such as factor analysis, it is good strategy to thoroughly acquaint oneself with the most simple methods before learning more subtle and involved aspects. It also is our belief that one of the best ways of accomplishing this is to apply it to actual data, and see the results. Therefore, it is essential that the reader begin by using existing computer programs to obtain some results as soon as possible.

Even if the reader does not yet have data to analyze, it is advisable to use some available computer program on hypothetical data, such as that shown in Table 9. Unfortunately, a problem in using existing programs is that they typically demand too many decisions for which the reader is not completely prepared. What we will demonstrate in this section is that there are many easy to use computer packages which are widely available, and that factor analysis programs included in these packages usually contain "default" options which require only a minimal number of decisions on the part of the user. As we have suggested several times, these default options are usually more than adequate, and, unless the user has a specific analysis problem that calls for a particular solution, it probably would be wise to rely on them.

The computer packages described and illustrated are limited to the following four widely available ones: BMD, OSIRIS, SAS, and SPSS. No endorsement of these packages over others is implied, and any program locally available can serve equally well. Before illustrating how these packaged programs can be used, it must be noted that each computer package has its own data handling system and set of control statements. We must assume that the potential user will study and learn these aspects of the system to be used. Therefore, what we show in these illustrations is not the entire set of control and specification statements, but only that portion which directly pertains to the factor analysis program.

ILLUSTRATION WITH SPSS

In using the factor analysis program, the user must specify: (1) the variables to be factor analyzed, (2) whether the data are in a raw form or in the form of a correlation or covariance matrix, (3) the number of common factors to be extracted or the criterion by which to determine such a number, (4) whether the diagonal elements of the correlation matrix are to be replaced by communality estimates and, if so, what type of estiates are to be used, (5) whether to employ orthogonal or oblique rotation, and (6) the particular type of rotation to be used.

We will first show how these choices are handled by the FACTOR program in SPSS. The simplest example of control cards in running factor analysis in which a minimum number of specifications are required of the user is as follows:

FACTOR   VARIABLES = VARA, VARC, VARF TO VARX/

STATISTICS   ALL

The first statement specified (through implied default options) the followint choices: (a) the variables to be included in the analysis are as listed in VARIABLES = list, (2) the input consists of raw data—that is, no correlation matrix has as yet been created, (3) the number of factors to be extracted is determined by the number of the roots (eigenvalues) of the correlation matrix which are greater than or equal to 1.0, (4) the communalities are estimated iteratively, (5) orthogonal rotation is to be used, and (6) the method of orthogonal rotation actually used is Varimax. The second statement will produce computer output consisting of the following items:

(1) means and standard deviations of all the variables included in the analysis;

(2) correlation matrix;

(3) inverse and determinant of the correlation matrix;

(4) unrotated (orthogonal) initial-factor matrix;

(5) terminal orthogonal factor matrix, rotated by the Varimax method;

(6) factor-score coefficient matrix consisting of regression weights with which to construct factor scales;

(7) plot of rotated factors—a visual display of clustering of variables for each pair of factors.

If one wants to obtain a final solution based on an oblique rotation, the easiest specification would look as follows:

FACTOR   VARIABLES = VARA, VARC, VARF TO VARX/
                         ROTATE = OBLIQUE/

STATISTICS   ALL

The only additional specification is the inclusion of the ROTATE = OBLIQUE statement. This will produce a terminal solution based on a particular oblique rotation, Direct Oblimin (with DELTA value set at 0). The output from such an oblique rotation would contain in the place of point 5 above, an oblique pattern matrix, a structure matrix, and a matrix of correlations among the oblique factors. The plot (point 7 above) is not available for oblique rotations.

What should be obvious from the preceding illustration is that it is, indeed, easy (perhaps too easy for the purists to feel comfortable) to do factor analysis with an existing program. We wish to reiterate that for the beginner to successfully use an existing program, unnecessary complications associated with the many possible choices should be avoided. Most of the options not mentioned in our illustration are purely technical ones that do not bear on the basic properties of factor analysis.

ADDITIONAL ILLUSTRATIONS WITH SPSS, BMD, OSIRIS AND SAS

As in SPSS, the other popular computer packages, such as BMD, OSIRIS and SAS contain factor analysis programs that offer many standard default options. We will first illustrate for SPSS and BMD, the way to obtain the maximum likelihood solution with oblique rotation. In addition, we will assume that the input is a matrix of correlations. The user should have little trouble in generaliziang from this to other options.

The simplest way to obtain such a solution with SPSS is to specify the following:

```
FACTOR      VARIABLES = list/
            METHOD = RAO/
            ROTATE = OBLIQUE/
```

The current version of SPSS handles the maximum likelihood solution by way of Rao's cannonical factoring technique; the default oblique rotation specifies a Direct Oblimin (with Delta equal to zero). The fact that the input is a correlation matrix is handled through an OPTIONS card and modifications in Job Control Language statements (not explained here).

The same maximum likelihood solution with oblique rotation starting with the correlation matrix is obtained in BMD (BMDP4M) as follows:

```
PROB/
INPUT      VARIAB=6. FORMAT='(6F4.3)'. CASE=100. TYPE=CORR./
FACTOR     NUMBER=2. METHOD=MLFA./
ROTATE     METHOD=DOBLI./
END/
```

The first card is the problem card which can be used to name the run. The default option assumes that nothing is specified, but the card is required anyway. The slash indicates the end of the card. The input card specifies the number of variables, format of the correlation matrix, size of sample on which the matrix is based, and the nature of the data—in this case, a correlation matrix. By changing CORR to DATA one can input raw data, and by changing CORR to COVA, one can input a covariance matrix. The factor card specifies the number of factors requested and the method of extraction—the maximum likelihood solution. The rotate card indicates a Direct Oblimin (with default gamma value = 0). As is evident, specifying control cards for the factor analysis program in BMD is almost as easy as in SPSS.

As of this writing, OSIRIS and SAS do not contain a maximum likelihood solution, but they contain many other standard extraction methods and a variety of rotation methods. We will illustrate each program package to show the ease with which a simple specification is possible.

An example using the OSIRIS package is as follows:

```
$RUN    FACTAN
AN ILLUSTRATION OF FACTOR ANALYSIS
*
SMR, ITER=20, OBLIMIN
*
$MATRIX
etc.
```

The first card specifies the program to be used; the second card is a label card—if deleted, the user has to insert a card containing *; the third card elects all the default specifications for the so-called global parameters— it indicates a matrix input form and what is referred to as the standard output; the fourth card specifies (a) that the number of variables analyzed is the same as the number of variables in the correlation matrix (by default), (b) the Kaiser criterion is used to determine the number of factors to be extracted (by default), (c) the initial estimates of communalities will be squared multiple Rs (by SMR), (d) these values will be iterated up to twenty cycles (by ITER = 20), (e) there will be no special output of factor scores or the pattern matrix (by default), and (f) the final solution will use (indirect) oblique rotation (by OBLIMIN). The next card with * on it specifies that all the default options in the oblique rotation will be chosen; for example, normalization of the factor matrix and use of the Biquartimin criterion. The last card, $MATRIX, specifies that information about the matrix follows. The "etc." means that the user must supply additional OSIRIS control cards for handling labels and input data.

An example of obtaining factor analysis through SAS is given below:

```
PROC    FACTOR    METHOD=PRINIT MINEIGEN=1    ROTATE=PROMAX
```

This statement specifies the choice of initial factoring based on principal axis factoring with iterations (PRINIT); the criterion of determining the number of factors is the Kaiser criterion; and the method of rotation is oblique PROMAX, which also implies that the initial rotation is done through Varimax. Data input and characteristics are described in other control cards which are not easy to describe without going into details of how SAS handles its input in general.

Complications in Analyzing Real Data

In the previous sections, we illustrated the application of factor analysis to error free data, and the general computer programs with which to obtain basic solutions. We concentrated on obtaining a solution while completely ignoring various complications that might arise. We must acknowledge, however, that the data one normally has will not fit the factor analysis model exactly. This is so because the data we usually analyze are not error free—they are subject to not only sampling and measurement errors but also to selection bias and disturbances created by minor factors not fully anticipated by the researcher. The computer programs we have introduced in the preceding section take these complications into account to a certain extent in obtaining a given solution, but some aspects of these complications are of an extra-statistical nature. For a fuller appreciation of factor analysis, the user must have at least a minimal degree of understanding of these complications. They are described below.

SAMPLING VARIABILITY

The correlation matrices we use as raw data for factor analysis are almost always based on sample data. Therefore, for any given sample, an observed correlation will never exactly reflect the underlying population correlation. The deviation from the underlying correlation matrix will be less as sample size increases, but even with a sample size, say 1,000, there can be substantial deviations for some correlations. One typical sample (to be precise, it is "typical" only in the sense that it happens to be the first random sample we have generated) of size 100 from the population model specified in Figure 16 and Table 9 is presented in the upper triangle of Table 14. Other sample results with the same size are presented in the lower triangle of Table 14.

By comparing these values with those shown in Table 9, and comparing the values in the upper triangle with the values in the lower triangle, you will notice that there is substantial variation from one table to another.

TABLE 14
**Correlations for Variables from two Samples of Size 100
from the Same Mother Population: The Upper Triangle Represents
a Different Sample from the Lower Triangle**

	x_1	x_2	x_3	x_4	x_5	x_6
x_1	--	.6008	.4984	.1920	.1959	.3466
x_2	.5461	--	.4749	.2196	.1912	.2979
x_3	.4734	.4284	--	.2079	.2010	.2445
x_4	.1119	.1625	.0673	--	.4334	.3197
x_5	.0387	.1348	.0275	.3804	--	.4207
x_6	.2639	.2070	.1597	.2817	.1543	--

a. The population correlations are given in Table 9.

Because factor analysis uses the correlation matrix as the data, we may infer that the result will be different when sample data are used and will vary across samples.

Because of this sampling variability one cannot rely completely on the rank-theorem presented in Section II. For instance, the rank-theorem that the reduced matrix will have a rank equal to the minimum of common factors compatible with the data will not hold exactly for any given sample. Likewise, there will be no way to replicate exactly the underlying communalities from the examination of a sample covariance matrix. Therefore, we will need either a general rule-of-thumb or some statistical test with which to test the adequacy of a particular solution based on sample data.

It can be said that almost all of the difficulties and complications in obtaining factor solutions are directly traceable to the computational difficulties in obtaining "good" estimates of underlying parameters by analyzing error-prone sample data. The logical problem of ascertaining the underlying causal (factor) structure from the examination of the covariance structure is more fundamental (as we have emphasized previously), but the resolution of that issue is handled by extra-statistical means and is not the major source of any computational complications. We will discuss the computational problems and their resolution more fully in the companion volume, when we describe various statistical methods of extracting factors.

We merely note at this point that with error free data (no sampling and measurement errors), a good factor analysis program should be able to

TABLE 15
Maximum Likelihood Two-Common Factor Solution Applied
to Data in the Upper Triangle of Table 14

Variables	Unrotated F_1	F_2	Communality	Rotated Using Direct Oblimin Criterion F_1	F_2
X_1	.747	-.300	.648	.817	-.027
X_2	.701	-.266	.562	.754	-.009
X_3	.599	-.176	.389	.602	.046
X_4	.428	.362	.314	.027	.547
X_5	.505	.605	.621	-.113	.833
X_6	.534	.248	.367	.202	.468
Sum of Squares[a]	2.132	.749		1.652	1.215
χ^2 with 4 degrees of freedom =	.825				

a. Sums of squares are equivalent to eigenvalues in the unrotated solution and this value divided by n gives the proportion of variance explained by that factor. In an obliquely rotated solution, they represent merely what might be called a "direct" contribution of each factor. The joint contribution (including that due to the correlation between the factors) is still equivalent to the sum of eigenvalues in the unrotated solution.

identify exactly the underlying simple factor structure. For instance, if we use the correlation matrix in Table 9, an extraction method based on either the maximum likelihood solution or the principal axis with iterated communalities solution, and final rotation based on the Direct Oblimin (with delta = 0), we should reproduce without error the known factor structure as shown in Figure 16. This cannot be expected when applied to sample data, however. To illustrate this, we have shown a terminal solution based on the maximum likelihood method and Direct Oblimin rotation as applied to the sample correlation matrix in the upper triangle of Table 14. (See Table 15.) This can be compared with Table 13.

SELECTION BIAS

In applying factor analysis, the most important decision is often made before the analysis, when the researcher selects variables to examine. Selection is invariably involved regardless of whether one designs a factor

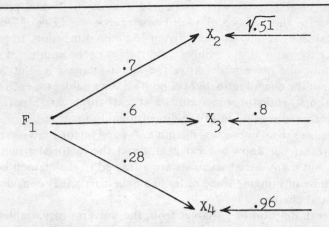

Figure 18: One Common-Factor Model Fit to a Subset of Variables from Table 9

analytic experiment or whether one takes a subset of variables from the existing survey. It will be difficult for any researcher to argue that a given set of items or variables constitutes the universe of all potential variables.
. Once we admit that we always deal with a certain subset of items out of a potentially large universe of items, we must worry about the possible selection bias. Let us first examine some simple but dramatic examples. Consider a situation in which the researcher examines only three variables, say, X_2, X_3, and X_4, from the model shown in Figure 16. Suppose for heuristic purposes that there are no measurement or sampling errors; we would then get the correlation matrix in which $r_{23} = .420$, $r_{24} = .196$, and $r_{34} = .168$ (i.e., a submatrix out of Table 9).

The application of a one-common factor model to this matrix would result in the factor structure shown in Figure 18, which may be compared with Figure 16. Not only does the factor loading (and communality and uniqueness) for X_4 change, but also the fact that X_4 belongs to a different dimension than X_2 and X_3 is completely lost. This example is not adequate for illustrating this argument, however, because it capitalizes also on the fact that applying a factor model to a three variable matrix is not terribly informative. Many (but not all) arbitrary three variable correlation matrices will exactly fit a one-common factor model as long as the magnitude of one correlation is not less than the magnitude of the product of the remaining two correlations.

Let us therefore consider examining the first four variables from the model shown in Figure 16. If there is no sampling error, one-common factor will completely account for the observed correlations as before.

This is an invalid result when evaluated against the model presumed known, but in the absence of such knowledge it would have led us to believe that there is only one underlying common dimension. In general, the greater the ratio of the number of variables to the number of underlying factors, the more informative the factor analysis is. But what is crucial is not the overall ratio, but the number of variables for each factor. Some authors (Thurstone) recommend at least three variables for each factor for a good resolution of the dimensionality issue.

This leads us to an interesting dilemma. A good factor analysis requires that the researcher know a great deal about the factorial structure of variables, but many social scientists are attracted to the method because of its promise of bringing some order to a data matrix they consider to be complex and chaotic.

In general, deletion of variables from the universe of variables for a factor model *can* affect the identification of that model. For this reason, most factor analysis methods (except *image* analysis) assume that there is no sampling of variables. The implications of violating this assumption are more serious than it might first seem. In fact, anyone who uses factor analysis is likely to run into a problem of selecting variables (inclusion as well as deletion of variables). On the one hand, inclusion of "unrelated" variables is often scorned by a harsh statement such as "Garbage in, garbage out." On the other, deletion of variables in order to have a neat factorial structure can lead into an erroneous conclusion. What we want to emphasize here is that no researcher can avoid making a certain number of judgmental decisions. An awareness of the assumptions required to use factor analysis is one of the key ingredients leading to sounder decisions.

MEASUREMENT ERRORS

The data we obtain are also subject to measurement error. If the measuring instrument is systematically biased (the errors are correlated), there is no easy way to solve the problem. But factor analysis can accommodate random measurement errors without too much problem. When random measurement error is considered, it is often treated as part of the unique factors. For example, a simple three variable one-common factor model with random measurement error can be represented as in Figure 19. Note that the variance of an observed variable is now decomposed into three parts:

$$\text{Var}(X_i) = (\text{Variance}) + (\text{Variance due to specific factor } S_i) \quad [35]$$
$$\text{due to } F_1$$
$$+ (\text{Measurement Error } E_i) = b_i^2 + s_i^2 + e_i^2$$

The effect of random measurement error is to lower the expected magnitude of correlations among variables. Some factoring methods, principal axis factoring, and to some extent Alpha factoring, try to incorporate the random measurement error component.

When there is random measurement error, it is possible to factor a correlation matrix that is corrected for attenuation, provided the reliability of each variable is known. However, there are several complications to deal with. First, correcting for attentuation for each correlation coefficient may lead to a matrix that is not Gramian (i.e., some of the characteristic roots associated with such a matrix may be negative; see Bock and Petersen [1975] for a discussion of multivariate correlation of attenuation). Second, the estimates of reliabilities themselves are also subject to sampling variability. Third, usually, the estimates of reliabilities are not available. In short, correcting for attenuation should not be viewed as always appropriate.

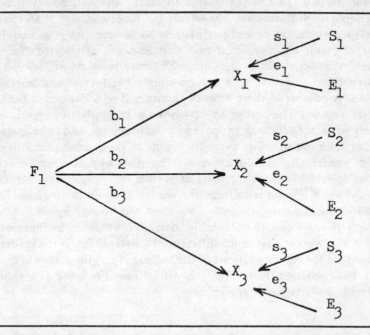

Figure 19: Simple One-Common Factor Model with Random Measurement Errors,

where $\mathrm{Var}(X_1) = b_1^2 + s_i^2 + e_i^2$, F = common factor, S_i = specific factor, E_i = random error component. (Unique factor = $U_i = S_i + E_i$.)

MINOR FACTORS

The problem we wish to address here is different from a more fundamental problem that the factor analytic model may not fit the data at all. We assume at this point that the factor analytic model is, in general, applicable to the data at hand. What is at issue is that in addition to a few major factors there may be some minor factors which do not contribute *substantially* to the covariance structure among the observed variables but are *statistically significant* given a large enough sample size. Stated from a somewhat different perspective, the problem is that we may not be able to ascertain when a given minor deviation is really due to sampling variability or to the lack of exact fit.

To summarize this section, we wish to emphasize that contrary to the impressions a novice may obtain from glancing through seemingly complex statistical algorithms displayed in technical articles on factor analysis, there are numerous uncertainties which allow considerable judgmental discretion on the part of the user. Knowledge of this seemingly unguided freedom will undoubtedly leave the novice with an uncomfortable feeling. This is not unique to factor analysis, however; actual data analysis problems are almost always more complex than the well developed statistical procedures assume to be true. As a consequence, users of factor analysis often find that less well articulated "rules-of-thumb" that acknowledge the complexity may be relied on, instead of a well specified rule that is based on simple but formal and unrealistic models. A number of these rules-of-thumb will be addressed in the companion volume. The reader by now should be ready to appreciate the variety of factor solutions proposed in the literature, and to tolerate any lack of definitive solutions regarding some of the crucial questions.

The reader also should appreciate by now why another volume is needed in which various methods of extracting and rotating factors are introduced. While we encourage the reader to study the material introduced in the companion volume, we close this volume by paraphrasing Kaiser's dictum—that all the subtle variations in obtaining factor solutions do not really make that much difference (Kaiser, 1970). If the reader has grasped the logical foundations of the technique and the means of obtaining a basic solution, factor analysis will be found to serve as a valuable tool with many research applications.

NOTE

1. Mean and variance are defined here as descriptive statistics (they are not treated as estimates of underlying parameters) and only with respect to discrete distributions. This does not mean, however, that our discussion will be limited to discrete distributions. The expectation notation is not only more compact but has the advantage of being generalizable

to a continuous distribution. However, since it is not essential for the understanding of the subject, we will not repeat these definitions for a continuous distribution. Furthermore, it will be assumed throughout Section II that concepts are defined for the population, unless otherwise stated or implied in the context.

QUESTIONS PERTAINING TO BOOKS, JOURNALS, AND COMPUTER PROGRAMS

(a) *Are there any books or articles on factor analysis a novice can read and readily understand?*

Not really. Most require some technical background. However, the following are easier than the others: Rummel (1967); Schuessler (1971); Cattell (1952); Comrey (1973); Fruchter (1954).

(b) *What are the "next-level" books that the serious reader should consider examining?*

Harman (1976); Mulaik (1972); Lawley and Maxwell (1971).

(c) *What are the major journals which regularly publish articles on factor analysis?*

Psychometrika; British Journal of Mathematical and Statistical Psychology; Educational and Psychological Measurement.

(d) *What are some of the general purpose computer packages containing factor analysis programs?*

SPSS; OSIRIS; SAS; BMD.

(e) *What are the more specialized programs dealing with factor analysis that one should know about?*

Kaiser's—Little Jiffy, Mark IV; Sörbom & Jöreskog—COFAMM.

(f) *Where are the major simulation studies reported?*

Tucker, Koopman and Linn (1969); Browne (1968); Linn (1968); Hakstian (1971); Hakstian and Abell (1974).

(g) *Where can one find a good list of references?*

Each of the text books listed in question (b) above contain extensive references to the literature. For an even handier list, we have included in this volume all of the references cited in the companion volumes.

REFERENCES

ALWIN, D. F. (1973) "The use of factor analysis in the construction of linear composites in social research." Sociological Methods and Research 2:191-214.

ANDERSON, T. W. and H. RUBIN (1956) "Statistical inference in factor analysis." Proceedings of the Third Berkeley Symposium on Mathematical Statistics and Probability 5:111-150.

ASHER, H. (1976) Causal Modeling. Sage University Papers on Quantitative Applications in the Social Sciences, 07-003. Beverly Hills and London: Sage Pub.

BMDP-77: Biomedical Computer Programs (P-Series). W. J. Dixon, Series Editor, M. B. Brown, Editor 1977 edition. Los Angeles: Univ. of California Press, 1977.

BARGMANN, R. E. (1957) A Study of Independence and Dependence in Multivariate Normal Analysis. Mimeo Series No. 186. Chapel Hill, N.C.: Institute of Statistics.

BARTLETT, M. S. (1937) "The statistical conception of method factors." British Journal of Psychology 28:97-104.

BOCK, R. D. and R. E. BARGMANN (1966) "Analysis of covariance structure." Psychometrika 31:507-534.

BOCK, R. D. and M. LIEBERMAN (1970) "Fitting a response model for N dichotomously scored items." Psychometrika 26:347-372.

BOCK, R. D. and A. C. PETERSON (1975) "A multivariate correction for attenuation." Biometrika 62:673-678.

BROWNE, M. W. (1968) "A comparison of factor analytic techniques." Psychometrika 33:267-334.

COFAMM: Confirmatory Factory Analysis with Model Modification User's Guide. Sörbom, D. and Jöreskog, K. G. Chicago: National Educational Resources, Inc., 1976.

CARROLL, J. B. (1953) "Approximating simple structure in factor analysis." Psychometrika 18:23-38.

—— (1961) "The nature of data, or how to choose a correlation coefficient." Psychometrika 26:347-372.

CATTELL, R. B. (1952) Factor Analysis. New York: Harper and Bros.

—— (1965) "Factor analysis: an introduction to essentials. (I) the purpose and underlying models, (II) the role of factor analysis in research." Biometrics 21:190-215, 405-435.

—— (1966) Handbook of Multivariate Experimental Psychology. Chicago: Rand McNally.

—— and J. L. MUERLE (1960) "The 'maxplane' program for factor rotation to oblique simple structure." Educational and Psychological Measurement 20:269-290.

CHRISTOFFERSSON, A. (1975) "Factor analysis of dichotomized variables." Psychometrika 40:5-32.

COMREY, A. L. (1973) A First Course in Factor Analysis. New York: Academic Press.

CRONBACH, L. J. (1951) "Coefficient alpha and the internal structure of tests." Psychometrika 16: 297-334.

DUNCAN, O. D. (1966) "Path analysis: sociological examples." American Journal of Sociology 72:1-16.

EBER, H. W. (1966) "Toward oblique simple structure maxplane." Multivariate Behavioral Research 1:112-125.

FRUCHTER, B. (1954) Introduction to Factor Analysis. New York: Van Nostrand.

GREEN, B. F., Jr. (1976) "On the factor score controversy." Psychometrika 41:263-266.

GUILFORD, J. P. (1977) "The invariance problem in factor analysis." Educational and Psychological Measurement 37:11-19.

GUTTMAN, L. (1953) "Image theory for the structure of quantitative variates." Psychometrika 18:227-296.

—— (1954) "Some necessary conditions for common factor analysis." Psychometrika 19:149-161.

HAKSTIAN, A. R. (1971) "A comparative evaluation of several prominent methods of oblique factor transformation." Psychometrika 36:175-193.

—— and R. A. ABELL (1974) "A further comparison of oblique factor transformation methods." Psychometrika 39:429-444.

HARMAN, H. H. (1976) Modern Factor Analysis. Chicago: University of Chicago Press.
———— (in press) "Minres method of factor analysis," in K. Enstein, A. Ralston, and H. S. Wilf (eds.) Statistical Methods for Digital Computers. New York: John Wiley.
———— and W. H. JONES (1966) "Factor analysis by minimizing residuals (Minres)." Psychometrika 31:351-368.
HARMAN, H. H. and Y. FUKUDA (1966) "Resolution of the Heywood case in the Minres solution." Psychometrika 31:563-571.
HARRIS, C. W. (1962) "Some Rao-Guttman relationships." Psychometrika 27: 247-263.
———— (1967) "On factors and factor scores." Psychometrika 32: 363-379.
———— and H. F. KAISER (1964) "Oblique factor analytic solutions by orthogonal transformations." Psychometrika 29:347-362.
HENDRICKSON, A. E. and P. O. WHITE (1964) "Promax: A quick method for rotation to oblique simple structure." British Journal of Mathematical and Statistical Psychology 17:65-70.
HORN, J. L. (1965) "An empirical comparison of various methods for estimating common factor scores." Educational and Psychological Measurement 25:313-322.
HORST, P. (1965) Factor Analysis of Data Matrices. New York: Holt Rinehart and Winston.
HOTELLING, H. (1933) "Analysis of a complex of statistical variables into principal components." Journal of Education Psychology 24:417-441, 498-520.
HOWE, W. G. (1955) Some Contributions to Factor Analysis. Report No. ORNL-1919. Oak Ridge, Tenn.: Oak Ridge National Laboratory. Ph.D. dissertation, University of North Carolina.
JENNRICH, R. I. (1970) "Orthogonal Rotation Algorithms." Psychometrika 35:229-235.
———— (1974) "Simplified formulae in standard errors in maximum likelihood factor analysis." British Journal of Mathematical and Statistical Psychology 27:122-131.
JENNRICH, R. I. and P. F. SAMPSON (1966) "Rotation for simple loadings." Psychometrika 31:313-323.
JÖRESKOG, K. G. (1963) Statistical Estimation in Factor Analysis: A New Technique and Its Foundation. Stockholm: Almquist and Wiksell.
———— (1966) "Testing a simple structure hypothesis in factor analysis." Psychometrika 31:165-178.
———— (1967) "Some contributions to maximum likelihood factor analysis." Psychometrika 32:443-482.
———— (1969) "A general approach to confirmatory maximum likelihood factor analysis." Psychometrika 34:183-202.
———— (1970) "A general method for analysis of covariance structure." Biometrika 57:239-251.
———— (1976) Analyzing Psychological Data by Structural Analysis of Covariance Matrices. Research Report 76-9. University of Uppsala, Statistics Department.
JÖRESKOG, K. G. and D. N. LAWLEY (1968) "New methods in maximum likelihood factor analysis." British Journal of Mathematical and Statistical Psychology 21:85-96.
KAISER, H. F. (1958) "The varimax criterion for analytic rotation in factor analysis." Psychometrika 23:187-200.
———— (1963) "Image analysis," pp. 156-166 in C. W. Harris (ed.) Problems in Measuring Change. Madison: University of Wisconsin Press.
———— (1970) "A second-generation Little Jiffy." Psychometrika 35:401-415.
———— (1974) "Little Jiffy, Mark IV." Educational and Psychological Measurement 34: 111-117.
———— (1974) "An index of factorial simplicity." Psychometrika 39:31-36.
KAISER, H. F. and J. CAFFREY (1965) "Alpha factor analysis." Psychometrika 30:1-14.
KIM, J. O. (1975) "Multivariate analysis of ordinal variables." American Journal of Sociology 81:261-298.

———— and C. W. MUELLER (1976) "Standardized and unstandardized coefficients in causal analysis: An expository note." Sociological Methods and Research 4:423-438.

KIM, J. O., N. NIE and S. VERBA (1977) "A note on factor analyzing dichotomous variables: the case of political participation." Political Methodology 4:39-62.

KIRK, D. B. (1973) "On the numerical approximation of the bivariate normal (tetrachoric) correlation coefficient." Psychometrika 38:259-268.

LISREL III: Estimation of Linear Structural Equation Systems by Maximum Likelihood Methods. (User's Guide). Jöreskog, K. G. and Sörbom, D. Chicago: National Educational Resources, Inc., 1976.

LITTLE JIFFY, MARK IV. (See Kaiser, 1974)

LABOVITZ, S. (1967) "Some observations on measurement and statistics." Social Forces 46:151-160.

———— (1970) "The assignment of numbers to rank order categories." American Sociological Review 35:515-524.

LAND, K. O. (1969) "Principles of path analysis," pp. 3-37 in E. F. Borgatta (ed.) Sociological Methodology. San Francisco: Jossey-Bass.

LAWLEY, D. N. (1940) "The estimation of factor loading by the method of maximum likelihood." Proceedings of the Royal Society of Edinburgh 60:64-82.

———— and MAXWELL, A. E. (1971) Factor Analysis as a Statistical Method. London: Butterworth and Co.

LEVINE, M. S. (1977) Canonical Analysis and Factor Comparison. Sage University Papers on Quantitative Applications in the Social Sciences, 07-006. Beverly Hills and London: Sage Pub.

LI, C. C. (1975) Path Analysis—A Primer. Pacific Grove, Calif.: Boxwood Press.

LINN, R. L. (1968) "A Monte Carlo approach to the number of factors problems." Psychometrika 33:37-71.

LORD, F. M. and W. R. NOVICK (1968) Statistical Theories of Mental Test Scores. Reading, Mass.: Addison-Wesley.

MALINVAND, E. (1970) Statistical Methods of Econometrics. New York: Elsevier.

MAXWELL, A. E. (1972) "Thomson's sampling theory recalled." British Journal of Mathematical and Statistical Psychology 25:1-21.

McDONALD, R. P. (1970) "The theoretical foundations of principal factor analysis, canonical factor analysis, and alpha factor analysis." British Journal of Mathematical and Statistical Psychology 23:1-21.

———— (1974) "The measurement of factor indeterminacy." Psychometrika 39:203-221.

———— (1975) "Descriptive axioms for common factor theory, image theory and component theory." Psychometrika 40:137-152.

———— (1975) "A note on Rippe's test of significance in common factor analysis." Psychometrika 40:117-119.

———— and E. J. BURR (1967) "A comparison of four methods of constructing factor scores." Psychometrika 32:380-401.

MULAIK, S. A. (1972) The Foundations of Factor Analysis. New York: McGraw-Hill.

NEUHAUS, J. O. and C. WRIGLEY (1954) "The method: an analytic approach to orthogonal simple structure." British Journal of Mathematical and Statistical Psychology 7:81-91.

OSIRIS Manual. Ann Arbor, Mich.: Inter-University Consortium for Political Research, 1973.

RAO, C. R. (1955) "Estimation and test of significance in factor analysis." Psychometrika 20:93-111.

RUMMEL, R. J. (1967) "Understanding factor analysis." Conflict Resolution 11:444-480.

———— (1970) Applied Factor Analysis. Evanston: Northwestern University Press.

SAS: A User's Guide to SAS 76. Anthony J. Barr, James H. Goodnight, John P. Sall, and Jane T. Helwig. Raleigh, N.C.: SAS Institute, Inc., 1976.

SPSS: Statistical Package for the Social Sciences. Norman H. Nie, C. Hadlai Hull, Jean G. Jenkins, Karin Steinbrenner, and Dale Bent. New York: McGraw-Hill, 1975.

SAUNDERS, D. R. (1953) An Analytic Method for Rotation to Orthogonal Simple Structure. Research Bulletin 53-10. Princeton, N.J.: Educational Testing Service.

——— (1960) "A computer program to find the best-fitting orthogonal factors for a given hypothesis." Psychometrika 25:199-205.

SCHUESSLER, K. (1971) Analyzing Social Data. Boston: Houghton Mifflin.

SÖRBOM, D. and K. G. JÖRESKOG (1976) COFAMM: Confirmatory Factor Analysis with Model Modification User's Guide. Chicago: National Educational Resources, Inc.

STEPHENSON, W. (1953) The Study of Behavior. Chicago: The University of Chicago Press.

STEVENS, S. S. (1946) "On the theory of scales of measurement." Science 103:677-680.

STINCHCOMBE, A. L. (1971) "A heuristic procedure for interpreting factor analysis." American Sociological Review 36:1080-1084.

THOMPSON, G. H. (1934) "Hotelling's method modified to give Spearman's g." Journal of Educational Psychology 25:366-374.

THURSTONE, L. L. (1947) Multiple Factor Analysis. Chicago: University of Chicago Press.

TRYON, C. R. and BAILEY, D. E. (1970) Cluster Analysis. New York: McGraw-Hill.

TUCKER, L. R. (1966) "Some mathematical notes on three mode factor analysis." Psychometrika 31:279-311.

——— (1971) "Relations of factor score estimates to their use." Psychometrika 36:427-436.

———, R. F. KOOPMAN, and R. L. LINN (1969) "Evaluation of factor analytic research procedures by means of simulated correlation matrices." Psychometrika 34:421-459.

TUCKER, L. R. and C. LEWIS (1973) "A reliability coefficient for maximum likelihood factor analysis." Psychometrika 38:1-8.

VELICER, W. F. (1975) "The relation between factor scores, image scores, and principal component scores." Educational and Psychological Measurement 36:149-159.

WAINER, H. (1976) "Estimating coefficients in linear models: it don't make no nevermind." Psychological Bulletin 83:213-217.

WANG, M. W. and J. C. STANLEY (1970) "Differential weighing: a review of methods and empirical studies." Review of Educational Research 40:663-705.

GLOSSARY

ALPHA FACTORING: a method of initial factoring in which the variables included in the analysis are considered samples from a universe of variables; see Kaiser and Caffrey in the references.

ADJUSTED CORRELATION MATRIX: the correlation matrix in which the diagonal elements are replaced by communalities; also used to refer to correlation or covariance matrices which are altered in a variety of ways before extracting factors.

BIQUARTIMIN CRITERION: a criterion applied in obtaining an indirect oblique rotation.

COMMUNALITY (h^2): the variance of an observed variable accounted for by the common factors; in an orthogonal factor model, it is equivalent to the sum of the squared factor loadings.

COMMON PART: that part of an observed variable accounted for by the common factors.

COMMON FACTOR: unmeasured (or hypothetical) underlying variable which is the source of variation in at least two observed variables under consideration.

CONFIRMATORY FACTOR ANALYSIS: factor analysis in which specific expectations concerning the number of factors and their loadings are tested on sample data.

CORRELATION: a measure of association between two variables; generally assumed to be the product-moment r (or Pearson's r); equivalent to the covariance between two standardized variables; also used as a general term for any type of linear association between variables.

COVARIATION: a crude measure of the degree to which two variables co-vary together; measured as the sum of cross-products of two variables which are expressed as deviations from their respective means; also used as a general term for describing the association between variables.

COVARIANCE: a measure of association between two variables; covariation divided by the number of cases involved; expected value of the sum of cross-products between two variables expressed as deviations from their respective means; the covariance between standardized variables is also known as the correlation.

COVARIANCE-STRUCTURE ANALYSIS: an analysis strategy (1) in which the observed covariance is expressed in terms of a very general model which can accommodate hypothetical factors as well as observed variables, and (2) in which the researcher then specifies appropriate parameters to evaluate the adequacy of the specification against the sample covariance structure.

COVARIMIN: a criterion for obtaining an oblique rotation; a variant of indirect oblimin rotation.

DETERMINANT: a mathematical property of a square matrix; discussed as a means of determining the rank (or the number of independent dimensions) of an adjusted correlation matrix.

DIRECT OBLIMIN: a method of oblique rotation in which rotation is performed without resorting to reference axes.

EIGENVALUE (or characteristic root): a mathematical property of a matrix; used in relation to the decomposition of a covariance matrix, both as a criterion of determining the number of factors to extract and a measure of variance accounted for by a given dimension.

EIGENVECTOR: a vector associated with its respective eigenvalue; obtained in the process of initial factoring; when these vectors are appropriately standardized, they become factor loadings.

EQUIMAX: a criterion for obtaining an orthogonal rotation; this criterion is a compromise between varimax and quartimax criteria.

ERROR-FREE DATA: contrived data where the underlying model is presumed known and there is an exact fit between data and model.

EXPECTATION: a mathematical operation through which the mean of a random variable is defined for both discrete and continuous distributions; an expected value is the property of a particular variable.

EXPLORATORY FACTOR ANALYSIS: factor analysis which is mainly used as a means of exploring the underlying factor structure *without* prior specification of number of factors and their loadings.

EXTRACTION OF FACTORS OR FACTOR EXTRACTION: the initial stage of factor analysis in which the covariance matrix is resolved into a smaller number of underlying factors or components.

ERROR COMPONENT: the part of the variance of an observed variable that is due to random measurement errors; constitutes a portion of the unique component.

FACTORS: hypothesized, unmeasured, and underlying variables which are presumed to be the sources of the observed variables; often divided into unique and common factors.

FACTOR LOADING: a general term referring to a coefficient in a factor pattern or structure matrix.

FACTOR PATTERN MATRIX: a matrix of coefficients where the columns usually refer to common factors and the rows to the observed variables; elements of the matrix represent regression weights for the common factors where an observed variable is assumed to be a linear combination of the factors; for an orthogonal solution, the pattern matrix is equivalent to correlations between factors and variables.

FACTOR SCORE: the estimate for a case on an underlying factor formed from a linear combination of observed variables; a by-product of the factor analysis.

FACTOR STRUCTURE MATRIX: a matrix of coefficients where the coefficients refer to the correlations between factors and variables; it is equivalent to a pattern matrix in the orthogonal case.

FACTORICAL COMPLEXITY: a characteristic of an observed variable; the number of common factors with (significant) loadings on that variable.

FACTORIAL DETERMINATION: the overall degree to which variations in observed variables are accounted by the common factors.

GRAMIAN: a square matrix is Gramian if it is symmetrical and all of the eigenvalues associated with the matrix are greater than or equal to zero; unadjusted correlation and covariance matrices are always Gramian.

IMAGE FACTORING: a method of obtaining initial factors; the observed variation is deomposed into (partial) images and anti-images, instead of into common parts and unique parts.

KAISER CRITERION: a criterion of determining the number of factors to extract; suggested by Guttman and popularized by Kaiser; also known as the "eigenvalue greater than one" criterion.

LINEAR COMBINATION: a combination in which variables are combined with only constant weights.

LINEAR SYSTEM: relationship among variables referred to as a whole, in which all the relationships are linear; factor analysis model in which all of the variables are assumed to be linear functions of underlying factors.

LEAST-SQUARES SOLUTION: in general, a solution which minimizes the squared deviations between the observed values and predicted values; a method of extracting initial factors, whose variants include principal axis factoring with iterated communalities and Minres.

MAXIMUM LIKELIHOOD SOLUTION: in general, a method of statistical estimation which seeks to identify the population parameters with a maximum likelihood of generating the observed sample distribution; a method of obtaining the initial factor solution; its variants include canonical factoring (RAO) and a method that maximizes the determinant of the residual partial correlation matrix.

MONTE CARLO EXPERIMENT: a strategy whereby various sample properties based on complex statistical models are simulated.

OBLIMAX: a criterion for obtaining an oblique rotation: it is equivalent to the quartimax criterion in orthogonal rotation.

OBLIMIN: a general criterion for obtaining an oblique rotation which tries to simplify the pattern matrix by way of reference axes; its variants include bi-quartimin, covarimin, and quartimin.

OBLIQUE FACTORS: factors that are correlated with each other; factors obtained through oblique rotation.

OBLIQUE ROTATION: the operation through which a simple structure is sought; factors are rotated without imposing the orthogonality condition and resulting terminal factors are in general correlated with each other.

ORTHOGONAL FACTORS: factors that are not correlated with each other; factors obtained through orthogonal rotation.

ORTHOGONAL ROTATION: the operation through which a simple structure is sought under the restriction that factors be orthogonal (or uncorrelated); factors obtained through this rotation are by definition uncorrelated.

PRINCIPAL AXIS FACTORING: a method of initial factoring in which the adjusted correlation matrix is decomposed hierarchically; a principal axis factor analysis with iterated communalities leads to a least-squares solution of initial factoring.

PRINCIPAL COMPONENTS: linear combinations of observed variables, possessing properties such as being orthogonal to each other, and the first principal component representing the largest amount of variance in the data, the second representing the second largest and so on; often considered variants of common factors, but more accurately they are contrasted with common factors which are hypothetical.

POSTULATE OF FACTORIAL CAUSATION: the assumption that the observed variables are linear combinations of underlying factors, and that the covariation between observed variables is solely due to their common sharing of one or more of the common factors.

[79]

POSTULATE OF PARSIMONY: this stipulates that, given two or more equally compatible models for the given data, the simpler model is believed to be true; in factor analysis, only the model involving the minimum number of common factors is considered appropriate.

QUARTIMAX: a criterion for obtaining an orthogonal rotation; the emphasis is on simplifying the rows of the factor pattern matrix.

QUARTIMIN: a criterion for obtaining an oblique rotation; the oblique counterpart of the quartimax rotation; requires the introduction of reference axes.

RANK OF A MATRIX: the number of linearly independent columns or rows of a matrix; the order of the largest square submatrix whose determinant is not zero.

REFERENCE AXES: these refer to axes that are orthogonal to the primary factors; they are introduced to simplify oblique rotation.

SCREE-TEST: a rule-of-thumb criterion for determining the number of significant factors to retain; it is based on the graph of roots (eigenvalues); claimed to be appropriate in handling disturbances due to minor (unarticulated) factors.

SIMPLE STRUCTURE: a special term referring to a factor structure with certain simple properties; some of these properties include that a variable has factor loadings on as few common factors as possible, and that each common factor has significant loadings on some variables and no loadings on others.

SPECIFIC COMPONENT: the part of the variance of an observed variable that is due to a factor which is specific to a given variable; used to designate the part of the unique component that is not due to random errors.

TARGET MATRIX: a matrix of coefficients used as a target in rotation; an initial factor solution may be rotated in such a way that the resulting factor loadings resemble the target matrix maximally.

VARIANCE: a measure of dispersion of a variable; defined as the sum of squared deviations from the mean divided by the number of cases or entities.

VARIATION: a measure of dispersion in a variable; loosely used as a general term for describing any type of dispersion around some central value; sum of squared deviations from the mean.

VARIMAX: a method of orthogonal rotation which simplifies the factor structure by maximizing the variance of a column of the pattern matrix.

UNIQUE COMPONENT: the part of the observed variance unaccounted for by the common factors; the proportion that is unique to each variable; it is often further decomposed into specific and error components.

UNIQUE FACTOR: the factor which is believed to affect only a single observed variable; often stands for all the independent factors (including the error component) that are unique to a variable.

JAE-ON KIM, *associate professor of sociology at the University of Iowa, received his undergraduate education at the Seoul National University, Korea, and his graduate degrees at Southern Illinois University and the University of California, Berkeley. He has published articles on quantitative methods and political sociology in such journals as* American Journal of Sociology, American Political Science Review, Sociological Methods and Research, *and* Political Methodology, *and his books include the recently coauthored (with Verba and Nie)* Participation and Political Equality: A Seven-Nation Comparison *(1978).*

CHARLES W. MUELLER, *associate professor of sociology at the University of Iowa, received his undergraduate education at Iowa State University and his Ph.D. from the University of Wisconsin-Madison. He has published articles on social stratification and quantitative methods in such journals as* American Sociological Review, Sociological Methods and Research, *and* Journal of Marriage and Family. *He is currently involved in research on organizational turnover and sex differences in social mobility.*